Nine Ways to Cross a River

Nine Ways to Cross a River

Midstream Reflections on Swimming and
Getting There from Here

AKIKO BUSCH

BLOOMSBURY

Published by Bloomsbury USA, New York
Distributed to the trade by Holtzbrinck Publishers

A portion of the introduction initially appeared, in slightly different form, in the
Harvard Review. "The Hudson River, September 5, 2004" was first published in a much
shorter form in *Metropolis* (December 2004), and the author is grateful for the
permission to include it here.

All papers used by Bloomsbury USA are natural, recyclable products made from wood
grown in well-managed forests. The manufacturing processes conform to the environmental regulations of the country of origin.

LIBRARY OF CONGRESS CATALOGING-IN-PUBLICATION DATA

Busch, Akiko.
Nine ways to cross a river : midstream reflections on swimming and
getting there from here / Akiko Busch.—1st U.S. ed.
p. cm.
ISBN-13: 978-1-59691-045-4 (alk. paper)
ISBN-10: 1-59691-045-3 (alk. paper)
1. Swimming—United States.   2. Rivers—United States.   3. Swimming—Philosophy.
I. Title.

GV838.53.P75B87 2007
797.2—dc22
2006030270

First U.S. Edition 2007

1 3 5 7 9 10 8 6 4 2

Typeset by Westchester Book Group
Printed in the United States of America by Quebecor World Fairfield

For the boys—Colin, Noel, Luc,
Sam, and Gabriel

Contents

You could not step twice into the same river;
for other waters are ever flowing on to you.

—Heraclitus

INTRODUCTION

The Hudson River

AUGUST 29, 2001

T HE FIRST POOL I ever swam in was a small cement pool in the
garden of my childhood home in Bangkok. I was three, my sister, five, and my father had decided we were of the age for swimming
lessons. He determined the pool's measurements by lying down on
the ground and having an oval drawn around him in chalk on the
grass, and then arranged for a shallow pool, not more than eighteen
inches deep, to be built conforming to that circle. Years later, when I
was in elementary school in upstate New York and first saw a print of
Leonardo da Vinci's Vitruvian Man, which delineated the propor-
tions of a human being with his legs spread and his arms out-
stretched, my reaction was one of delight: Here, I thought, is a man
who is planning on building a swimming pool for his daughters!

Since that time, or perhaps because of it, I have always drawn a connection between the dimensions of a human being and a good swimming pool. A river simply extends the equation. It only made sense, then, that swimming has always been a way to take measure of experience. So when it began to feel as though my life had become defined by a series of divides, it seemed to be the time to take a swim. A close friend had died. My own half-century mark was a couple of years down the road. And my sons, twelve-year-old twins, were in an adolescent landscape furnished with language, clothes, activities, all incomprehensible to me. For these, there was little to be done. Perhaps for that reason, the idea was growing on me: Find a divide that could be crossed. And more and more I realized, I wanted to swim across the Hudson River.

As a swimmer I have always looked to the Hudson River. I have lived in the Hudson Valley for much of my life, and the wide swath of river has always been at one edge of it or another. Besides, I am a strong believer in symbolic sports; I find an appeal in metaphorical exercise. Swimming across the river was a symbolic way of breaching the divide; it was about nothing more and nothing less than the possibility of getting there, somewhere, from here. And so for the course of one winter, as I did my laps at the local gym, I dreamed of swimming across the Hudson, imagining in the seventy-five-foot pool of tepid water the draw of the river current, the ancient tug of its tides. In *Theory of Colours*, his study of wavelength theory of light and color published in 1910, the German philosopher and writer Johann Wolfgang von Goethe said of the color blue, "But as we readily follow an agreeable object that flies from us, so we love to contemplate blue, not because it advances to us, but because it draws us after it." He could have been talking about rivers as much as he was talking about the color they sometimes are. And certainly, he could have been talking about the Hudson River, its color and its draw.

When summer came, I looked for more practical advice. My friends who live on the river all told me that the water temperature stayed cool until late summer, so August it would be. I tracked down Brian Kempf, a senior marine service representative at the New York State Office of Parks, Recreation and Historic Preservation in Albany. Kempf's manner was straightforward, his advice based on common sense. "Have someone with a guide boat," he said, as a precaution for any emergency and a way for other watercraft to steer clear. "And plan your swim for an early weekday morning, when there are fewer pleasure boats on the river," he added. "And make sure you schedule your swim for slack tide." But then his matter-of-factness dissolved into pure enthusiasm. "It sounds like a lot of fun," he said. "Have a great time."

While I had known that even some 150 miles north of its mouth the river remains susceptible to the tide, the changeable force of its alternating current always surprises me. For over a thousand years, the Algonquin called the river Muhheakantuck, which means "river that flows two ways," and indeed, the Hudson River is a paradox made manifest in the natural world: It flows to the north at times, to the south at other times. It is a curious sight on a winter's day to watch the ice floes on the river surge to the north, back toward the river's source rather than south toward the Atlantic Ocean; there is something mesmerizing about watching an event in the natural world unfold with such a contrary rhythm. Stranger still is watching the ice floes in the center of the river flow one way, while those on the edges flow in the opposite direction. Such spectacles seem to challenge every notion you have about the natural order of things, powerful evidence that our ideas of innate order are not always to be trusted.

John Cronin, former riverkeeper and now the executive director of the Beacon Institute for Rivers and Estuaries in Beacon, New York, explains the interaction between the current and the tide as "a matter of inertia." Because the bottom of the river, from its mouth to the Troy Dam some 150 miles north, is below sea level, the tidal force of the ocean causes the river to rise and fall; the river, in fact, is one continuous wave, which explains why the tide rises and falls at such different times at different points along the river. Even the word *river* verges on inaccuracy; were the freshwater from rain and snowfall that reaches the river to be eliminated, the Hudson would be an estuary. And while the current of the river flows with the tide, it is governed by its own inertia. Cronin uses the analogy of a passenger in a speeding car: When the car stops going forward, the passenger still continues to move forward. In much the same way, the current flows with the tide, but it continues to flow for an hour or so after high tide.

The position of the sun and moon, along with tidal surges, all add to the vagaries of the interaction between current and tide. So, too, does the fact that the current is faster in midriver, where it flows freely, and slower at the edges, where there is more obstruction. And there are parts of the river, too, where the width and the contours of its banks never permit the tide to slacken. "It's all counterintuitive," Cronin concludes. "You have to use logic to understand it. You have to rely on the basic facts of gravity and inertia. But even then it gets complex."

Jumping into a cool river on a hot summer day is a universally appealing proposition, and by late August, there were five of us: Emily, who was twenty-one and had just graduated from college that June; Myron, her father, who teaches school in Wallkill; Jon, an actor from New York City; and his wife, Onni. Their fourteen-year-old son, Sam, was with us too, but not being a swimmer, he came along for the boat ride. Carrie, a friend of Emily's, followed us in her father's twenty-three-foot Fiberglas powerboat, *Gross Envy*, moored in New Hamburg. High tide was at 10:32, and the tide would be slack for an hour or so after that.

We met at a scrap of small sandy beach near the marina in New Hamburg, a place where the river narrows. The village was built along a slight promontory that juts out into the Hudson, and the river isn't much more than a half mile wide. But distance across water is always difficult to gauge; here, the surface of the river was scalloped by the lightest morning breeze, and I could find no reliable measure for the distance. Only a destination; on the west bank of the river, directly across from us, was a thin ledge of dust-colored rock just below the railroad tracks, and at that moment, it was as good as an objective as any. We swam through the tangles of weeds that clogged the shallow water, then past the docks of the marina and into the wide expanse of the river itself.

As we swam out into the deeper channel, the water temperature dropped slightly. A slight surface current created by the wind seemed to tug south, but almost unbelievably, the tide being slack, there was no sense of any stronger pull beneath the surface, and the river that flows both ways seemed more a placid lake. In the middle of the river, one's perceptions of distance, motion, and time all seem slightly askew. Midriver is a place of suspension, and one is adrift in every sense. A pleasure boat cruised lazily up the river, but it stayed far to our south, seeming to drift in its own separate waterscape. I have lived in the Hudson Valley for most of my life, but immersed that morning in its essential artery, I felt I had finally acquired true citizenship.

It was not only the current and tide we were oblivious to; that there was a vast archive of marine history beneath us could only be imagined as well. During the late nineties, scientists initiated a program to use sonar to map the bed of the Hudson River. Believing that such a map would help to establish baseline data about marine habitat, vegetation, and the effects of pollution, they tracked the river floor using sound waves. In doing so, they also discovered evidence of some two hundred wrecks, everything from Revolutionary War vessels to overturned barges to nineteenth-century sloops, an entire catalog of river life. There is evidence of other human constructions as well, a nine-hundred-foot-long wall, for example, that dates back some three thousand years, when the river's low water level allowed for construction.

Because it contains almost no oxygen, the silt on the bottom of the river also serves as a preservative, and the researchers located everything from coal to fur and textiles, bricks to blueberries preserved at the river's bottom. The problem with this seemingly perfect archival material is that it does not allow for visibility. The river bottom is an extensive improvisational museum, cataloged but invisible, of value exactly because it hides as it accumulates. This inaccessibility is underscored by the fact that the sonar maps of the river floor remain unpublished. Both to preserve the submerged material and to discourage scavengers who might endanger themselves and disturb valuable research material, the precise whereabouts of these various wrecks remains known only to officials at the New York State Office of Parks, Recreation and Historic Preservation. Indeed, this vast collection remained unknown, unfelt, unseen even to a swimmer treading water directly above it. There are people, I know, who are apprehensive about swimming in rivers exactly because they cannot see and cannot know what's beneath them. But for me on this summer morning, to tread water lightly above the vestiges of these wrecks, their spilled cargo, and all the debris they have left is full of promise and possibility, reaffirming the fact that we live with the unknown in everything we do.

That the river is a place of industry was in ample evidence. To the north was a slow-moving tugboat pulling a series of barges from the Trap Rock Plant. From our midriver vantage point, it appeared to be its own distant little industrial village—the eight immense barges arranged in two rows of four. "What a bonus," Myron said. "This is our lucky day." The Trap Rock Plant just north of New Hamburg is one of the river's industrial landmarks. Its crusher, originally put to use in the construction of the Panama Canal, now crushes dolomite, an aggregate of concrete, taken from rock quarries on either side of the river, which is then shipped on barges to New York City for construction projects. It is common river lore that it takes such barges a good mile to come to a complete stop, and that, along with a distinct awareness of our inferior scale, encouraged us to tread water until it passed.

Not simply an industrial artery, the Hudson is a biologically productive river. The horizontal movement of the current and the vertical motion of the tides keep the water constantly mixing, silt continually churned, nutrients constantly stirred up. Not far upstream, scientists from the Institute of Ecosystem Studies have been researching the effects of this phenomenon on the river's aquatic life. In the late 1800s, the Eurasian water chestnut was introduced to the river. Trailing its slight, feathery tendrils, the plant's wide leaves rest on the surface of the water, limiting the amount of light into the water, thereby reducing the level of oxygen in the water and diminishing the possibility for photosynthesis. The question, then, is to what degree the dense beds of invasive water chestnut have compromised aquatic life and marine habitats. Gene Likens, the president and director of IES, tends to shrug and say, "It's all beneath the surface," a statement brilliant in its simple reduction.

That the Hudson should accommodate such diverse enterprises is part of its modern history. Even the painters of the Hudson River School sometimes found themselves in a quandary, divided as whether to render the river as a naturalist's Arcadia or acknowledge the intrusions of industry; often, they managed to do both, with picturesque plumes of smoke and compositionally correct railways that conformed to—rather than disrupted—the idyllic landscape. But what is even more common to so many of those paintings is how a single landscape can accommodate such a wide view of nature. One sees on a single canvas a foreground in which a farmer is tending his cattle or baling hay or a man fishing near a stream, scenarios of a docile and benign nature that allows itself to be harnessed for man's ordinary appetites. In the background, though, are the epic clouds and operatic sunsets, incandescent and sublime skycapes full of light that evoke a more spiritual experience. Even now, it is easy to understand these multiple personas of the natural world, because the Hudson River and the valley around it encourage such an extravagance of perception. The quiet activity of the New Hamburg marina and our own swim in the calm water were framed by the greater spectacle of the Hudson Highlands just downstream and the unfathomable expanse of an azure summer sky.

A century after the landscapes of the Hudson River School were painted, scholars in the newly minted field of environmental psychology suggested that our view of the rooms, the houses, the whole landscapes we inhabit gives us mental maps which are essential to the way we chart our course through life. In one textbook I read that "the validity of our perceptions, whether they work or not, has meaning to us only insofar as they help us perceive our purposes, help us attain those particular satisfactions of living for which each of us is striving. The overall function of environmental perception is not to reveal present reality, nor to recall past reality; rather, it is to predict the future. Perception is anticipatory." Certainly those painters must have believed that. Everywhere on their canvases is the conviction that man, god, and nature can reasonably accommodate one another. On this quiet summer morning, it was possible to believe that as well, and the five of us simply treaded water for ten or fifteen minutes, watching the slow crawl of the tug until it had passed. Not until the barges were well downriver did we resume our swim.

The water on the west side of the river seemed brackish. At that particular point on the shore there are no beaches or marinas, just the train tracks above the rock pilings; and moments later, as we sat on the rocks, a freight train rattled on the tracks above us. If distance across water is difficult to judge, so too is time. Half a mile, forty five-minutes were the numbers I imagined, but these were the lesser part of the calculation. With the barge chugging south, the pleasure boats drifting out from the marina, and now the train speeding south, our own little swim seemed but a part of the myriad enterprises generated by the river. And although we hadn't planned on it, that sense of enterprise, along with the gentle current, the play of light on water, the sheer pleasure of it all motivated us to swim back as well. Even Sam, until that moment a passenger on the boat, dove off *Gross Envy* into the water and joined us in the return trip. Weeks later, when I looked at a photograph of us arriving back at the marina, it was a small document of completion.

It was a good way to mark the end of the summer of 2001. Sam was beginning high school the next week, and Emily was considering graduate schools. Myron was preparing for a new class. The rest of us faced lesser passages. None of us that day had any idea how quickly the world would change. It has always been curious to me how we so often remember important events in our lives not by the logical progression of things that lead up to them or that emerge out of them, but to utterly unconnected events that may happen around them, or later; and how human memory is not only receptive to, but strangely appreciative of, random happenstance, associating disparate events with one another simply because they share proximity in time. Events, things seen, read, and heard all converge with one another, jumble around, then settle in comfortably with one another, their adjacency established. Certainly now I can no longer think of that late summer swim in 2001 without some knowledge of how different the world looked less than two weeks later. And though it didn't start out that way, when I think back now to that morning in late August, that short swim across a wide river imprinted itself on all of us as an image of possibilities realized. And for that reason, then, it became essential to mark each summer after that with a river crossing.

It's not so farfetched. Swimming in the Hudson River has a storied past. Robert Juet was an officer on the *Half Moon* when it took its excursion up the river in September 1609, and his journal records on the fifteenth of that month: "This morning out two savages got out of a Port and swam away. After we were under sayle, they called to us in scorne." Eight days later, Henry Hudson also observed the approach of natives, "some in their canoes, some swimming"; whether they too were scornful goes unnoted. In subsequent years, swimming in the Hudson tended to be done informally, and was informally recorded, usually a matter of kids jumping into the water wherever there was a pier or a barge that let them do so. In the late nineteenth and early twentieth centuries, amusement parks, boat clubs, and other recreation areas up and down the river offered urban residents respite from the debilitating summer heat. Add to that the floating pools built around the perimeter of Manhattan, and it's clear that swimming was a part of the social life along the river.

John Iurica is a retired engineer in Piermont who has lived on the Hudson all his life, and he has cataloged more recent river swimmers— from the Bluefield Bathers, a women's swimming group between the the world wars to swims from parks and amusement parks on the lower river before the Tappan Zee Bridge was built. He recalls one especially stalwart swimmer in Piermont in the forties and fifties, a woman who could "probably beat up any of the local fishermen. She would sit on a bench at the end of the pier and consume a six-pack of beer, while her friend also had a six-pack. She would then remove her clothes, having a bathing suit on underneath, dive in, and swim to the other side and back. If she felt like she needed to cool off some more, she would consume another six-pack, walk inland to Cornetta's Marina, dive in the river again, and swim back and forth over its three-mile width. There are people who have in recent years tried to get some publicity by swimming across the river and back. If they want to impress us locals, they should drink the twelve cans (or more) of beer first."

By the fifties, though, most people would have needed a lot more than a six-pack to be persuaded to get in the river. By the mid-twentieth century, many American rivers were biologically dead. If the growth of the American nation started on the banks of its rivers, which offered navigational arteries, provided irrigation for farms, and powered gristmills and sawmills, rivers were also a place to flush away agricultural and household waste. The factories and mills of the industrial age continued the tradition, exploiting the rivers' resources and their hydroelectric power, all the while dumping their own toxic waste into their waters. Often, and especially if a railroad track ran alongside the river, the riverbank was a narrow corridor of commerce that effectively separated communities from the rivers they were built on.

By the mid-nineteenth century, the Hudson River was an industrial landscape, providing bricks from its vast clay deposits, limestone, and cement for the construction of New York City; steamboats chugged upriver, and trains puffed alongside. The construction of a canal system that both connected the river to the Great Lakes and channeled water from upstate lakes and reservoirs for the city's water supply all fed even more traffic onto the river. On the Connecticut River, the industry of gristmills and timber logging gave way to factories for paper, firearms, tools, furniture, textiles, silverware, and shoes. By the early twentieth century, generations of industrial contaminants, agricultural waste, and household sewage had all taken their toll, degrading American riverways into a toxic brew inhospitable to any kind of direct human use or engagement. When I was a teenager, I would often take the train from my home up the river in Dutchess County to Manhattan, and the tracks passed by the auto plant in Tarrytown; for years I had heard that people who lived along that stretch of the river knew what color General Motors was painting its cars by the color of the river. More catastrophic were the polychlorinated biphenyls (PCBs), a man-made chemical invented in 1929; until they were banned in 1976, they were used as insulators, coolants, and lubricants on industries along the river. A stable chemical compound that is difficult to break down, PCBs, when dumped into the river, tend to concentrate in sediment, then travel up the food chain. A known cancer-causing chemical, it impairs the nervous, immune, and reproductive systems of whatever living organisms it comes in contact with.

President Lyndon Johnson enacted the National Wild and Scenic Rivers Act in 1968, articulating a new policy of protecting the scenery, recreational uses, geology, fish, and wildlife of American rivers—all the while balancing the need to construct dams for water supply and hydroelectric power. It was a tall order, but a start for the process of river regeneration and one reinforced by the passage of the Clean Water Act in 1972. The cleanup of the Hudson River is now well into its fourth decade. Since the sixties, a coalition of environmental activists has managed to block the construction of two nuclear power plants and two major highways; they have instituted conservation programs, created endowments, and brought numerous smaller polluters to justice. But that said, proposed environmental incursions on the river remain constant, and even in 2006, organizations such as Riverkeeper, Scenic Hudson, Hudson River Estuary Program, and Clearwater, along with national entities like the Sierra Club and myriad grassroots community alliances, are joining forces to continue to pursue legal routes to enforce a court order demanding that General Electric clean the river from its some thirty years of dumping 1.3 million pounds of PCBs into it. And although a two-hundred-mile stretch of the Hudson River has been a Superfund site—a place where toxic waste has been dumped and which the Environmental Protection Agency is obligated to restore—since 1984, its cleanup continues to be delayed; the 2005 start date established by the EPA has now been put off until 2007, and possibly even 2008. Cleaning the Hudson is a day-to-day, week-to-week endeavor. In spring 2005, a proposal to build an expansive industrial cement plant in the river hamlet of Greenport was voted down in Albany after years of community resistance. Yet only weeks later, a barge oblivious to markers charting the river's navigational channels ran aground at Diamond Reef near New Hamburg, resulting in a massive gasoline spill. In spring 2006, Riverkeeper notified Entergy Nuclear Northeast of its intent to sue for the latter's failure to tell the EPA of a hazardous leak at its Indian Point nuclear power plant. These are only brief anecdotes in the story of one river. Despite the passage of the Clean Water Act over thirty years ago, the renewal of American rivers is as continuous as the rivers themselves.

So I found that whatever sense of personal renewal comes in

swimming across a river, it is one that parallels the reclamation of the river itself; the small sense of restoration one inevitably feels on swimming in a river can't help but mirror the story of that river's own restoration. The Connecticut River was famously called "the best landscaped sewer in the nation" half a century ago, and for the better part of the twentieth century, high counts of coliform bacteria made it inhospitable to recreation; with environmental legislation that began in the sixties, it is once again a habitat to osprey, bald eagles, salmon. And while much of the upper Delaware River has been restored as a scenic river or designated recreation area that is carefully patrolled, the lower river continues to be plagued by the demands of new construction and industrial waste. On the upper Susquehanna River, water testing remains limited, and out-of-date municipal sewage treatment facilities are inadequate after heavy rains; while the river is a tourist destination for camping, fishing, hiking, and boating, swimming in many places on the river is actively discouraged. Acid mine residues and outdated sewage plants continue to plague the Monongahela as well, though in recent years, bass, catfish, and carp have again become more abundant.

Four summers and nine rivers later, I have come to realize that the divide I once wanted to breach is not simply personal. Certainly that is a part of it, but traveling to these rivers and swimming across them has also served to connect me to the rivers and their communities; becoming immersed in the water of these rivers has also inevitably immersed me in their greater stories of transformation and renewal. At nearly every river I went to, I sooner or later confronted the conviction that the river was too dirty to swim in. While in some cases the warning to stay out of the river came from a knowledgeable source, just as often it was a product of uninformed local lore; the idea that rivers are just too polluted to swim in has become deeply rooted in the popular imagination of the American people. It is one of my hopes here to propose an alternative conviction; to suggest that as rivers are reclaimed, so too can they be restored to a function they have long served in the human community as a place of personal renewal. I am certain most of us are receptive to this idea. Or hint, as Robert Frost might see it. The Vermont poet once observed: "How many times it thundered before Franklin took the hint! How many apples fell on Newton's head before he took the hint! Nature is always hinting at us. It hints over and over again. And suddenly we take the hint."

The environmental movement took the hint some forty years ago, but it faces different concerns as it progresses into the twenty-first century. In earlier generations, the renewal of our rivers was often a question of identifying polluters, enacting legislations, enforcing penalties. Today, it may depend on a different kind of activism; it may count less on watchdog organizations and more on redefining the everyday habits of American people. Pesticides, fertilizers, road salts all find their way into rivers; and as farmland gives way to asphalt and pavement continues to carpet the natural landscape, it becomes easier and easier for these unregulated and inexpensive contaminants to drain into the rivers. At the same time, invasive nonnative plant and animal species are entering rivers' ecosystems at an ever-accelerating rate, disrupting the balance that has existed for centuries. As the burden of cleaning our rivers falls less on a handful of negligent corporations and more into the domain of the general population, the success of reclamation efforts may depend on public perceptions of the river; how and where it resides in our imaginations. As vital as cleaning the rivers is our recognition of their changing status and our reversal of the collective perceptions about the hostile waters of American rivers. Part of river reclamation is reclaiming its place in our popular imagination.

An irony comes into play here, because just as we begin to take measures to reclaim these rivers, we may have to do something even more important, which is to safeguard their very existence. Our use of fossil fuels has caused the earth's surface temperature to rise approximately one degree Farenheit in the past century. The continuing rise in temperature will have a catastrophic effect on the patterns of wind and ocean current, the foundation and center of our entire climate system. Scientists who are constructing models for the effects of global climate change anticipate a reduction in river flow, and one model suggests that it is entirely possible that the volume of water in large rivers around the world may decrease by 10 to 20 percent in the next century. Again, the continuing stewardship of rivers can only be furthered by reinstating their rightful place in the minds' eye of our culture.

Doing so may, at times, seem gratuitous. It is our tendency to anthropomorphize much of the natural world, whether it is the weather, our household animals, or simply a tree shedding its leaves. It is possible for us to see ourselves in everything. And surely this is easy to do with a river. The writer William Least Heat-Moon puts it succinctly when he says, "A river—with its attendant cascades, eddies, boils, and whirlpools—is the most expressive aspect of a natural landscape, for nothing else moves so far, so broadly, so unceasingly, so demonstrably, and nothing else is so susceptible to personification and so much at the heart of our notions about life and death." It comes naturally to find some metaphor for human experience in the strength or flow or velocity of a river, to find the familiar in the sight of two rivers peaceably merging or to imagine a kinship in the way one river pours into another until it is no longer itself. It is easy to find inspiration in the resilience of a river as it is restored from a polluted stew to a clear running stream. But if we see ourselves in rivers, I suspect that we are also seeing something much larger than ourselves. And while making such associations may be the height of human egotism, I would suggest it is an indulgence that can have a positive outcome. If rivers are permitted to represent some element of personal mythology, that can only serve to strengthen our connection to them.

Dennis Chillemi is a police officer in Irvington, New York. For over a decade he has organized an annual swim across the Hudson River to raise funds for the MS Society. And every year he tells the several hundred swimmers who participate that swimming in the river inevitably confers a sense of ownership; and how that ownership will likely lead to some kind of stewardship. Such a view of ownership has resonance for other river communities around the country. Each river has its own identity, and it is one you come to know the way you come to know anything or anyone you love: You are captivated by the sight of it; you are taken with its spirit; you learn its personal history. And then, sooner or later, you acquaint yourself with its physical presence. Each river has its own feel, taste, texture, its own flow and velocity. The stewardship of rivers will only be furthered by the intimate knowledge of these qualities. John Iurica is certain that the Hudson River has medicinal powers in that it cures poison ivy rashes. "It only takes about half an hour of being in the water on a sandy bottom to get rid of the rash," he says, attributing the cure to the minerals in the water and the abrasive action of the sand. "Placing salts in water in your bathtub and soaking in it does not work," he adds. "I've tried it."

Most people I encountered as I was swimming these rivers usually responded with an understanding of the restorative powers of rivers, whether it is in curing poison ivy or soothing some less identifiable misery. An intuitive appreciation for rivers seems to come with being human. At the same time, people often greeted my endeavor with curiosity, bafflement even. The Delaware is not a particularly wide river. The Susquehanna is often shallow. The Connecticut River is calm, placid. Swimming across these rivers doesn't require much athletic skill or prowess. It's not what you would call a sports challenge. Most people are too well mannered to come right out and say it, but the question implicit in their eyes is usually something along the lines of "What's the challenge? What's so hard about that?" Or, in essence, "What's the big deal?"

It is easy to understand that reaction. It's not a big deal. In *River-Horse*, William Least Heat-Moon offers us an eloquent document of a river trip across the entire continental United States, from the Hudson

River to the Columbia River, during which portage is treated only as a final option. But he was on a boat. Christopher Swain swam the entire lengths of the Hudson, Columbia, and Charles rivers in an effort to promote river stewardship. And there are accounts of swimmers who cross the English Channel regularly. The stormy, ten-mile Cook Strait between the North and South islands of New Zealand is one of the fiercest challenges to distance swimmers, and Lynne Cox spent eleven years trying to secure permission from the Soviet Union, and when she did, swam across the Bering Strait, where the water temperature dropped to thirty-eight degrees. Swimmers who attempt the crossing from Cuba to the Florida Keys must position themselves in steel cages to protect themselves from sharks, and precisely calibrating the movements of the swimmer, cage, and escort boat is a part of planning the swim. The river crossings in this book share nothing with these feats of courage, stamina, and heroic endurance. Rather, they tap into a more common desire to make smaller, simpler passages with ordinary skill; they answer to the ordinary hope that the currents of these rivers can find their way back into the patterns of ordinary life.

I think back to the little concrete swimming pool my father had made for me and my sister by stretching out his arms and legs. Vitruvius, the Roman authority on architecture, suggested in the first century BC that the human body is a model of proportion because when one's arms and legs are fully extended, it fits into the perfect geometric form, the circle and the square. In the words of the historian Kenneth Clark, this simple proposition as illustrated centuries later by da Vinci gave Renaissance thinkers "the foundation of a whole philosophy . . . it seemed to offer exactly that link between sensation and order, between an organic and geometric sense of beauty, which was (and perhaps remains) the philosopher's stone of aesthetics." I wonder if it is that link between sensation and order that makes swimming across a body of water gratifying. I wouldn't imagine it the foundation of a whole philosophy, yet there is something about swimming, possibly because it requires a committed partnership between breathing and moving, that affirms one's sense of interior order. And it is possible, too, for such a sense of order to be extended. It is not such a long distance between the small sense of proportion one feels swimming across a river and the larger sense of fit that an entire community can find with the natural world when it is connected to the river running through it. Perception, I remind myself, is anticipatory.

That, anyway, is a reason to swim across a river, that sense of almost primal order and proportion that the river swims managed to confer, river after river, year after year. My own interior landscape began with that small swimming pool in a garden in Bangkok. I didn't realize during that first swim across the Hudson River a half century later quite how much all of these rivers would come to extend the boundaries of my own cognitive map. What began in a garden with tamarind, hibiscus, mango and flame trees, a fan-shaped banana tree and a thicket of bougainvillea took me to the Connecticut with its forests of birch and maple, the Mississippi with its cottonwoods and hickory, the Current with its groves of bamboo and white oak.

But even that small pool was a place of mixed messages, and I learned early that a body of water can be both a wellspring of pleasure and a place of contaminants. Just as it lingers in my mind as a childhood idyll, I also know that it may be where I contracted tuberculosis at the age of three. Though there was no precise way for my parents to know how their small daughter got the disease, they suspected it was from a gardener at the house whose own lungs were later found to host the bacterial infection and who was often found sneezing or coughing or spitting not far from the pool. Possibly this is a case of postcolonial assumption of the culpability of the locals. But possibly, also, it is true. To be in Southeast Asia in the early fifties with a young child with tuberculosis was frightening, and it was a contributing factor in my parents' decision to leave Thailand and return to the States, where better treatments were available.

Not long after, I was, of course, cured of TB. I heard someone say

once that "swimmers are people who wish they had never been born."
The statement has a kind of fatalistic and self-dramatizing appeal,
suggesting that people who are drawn to water never made a final,
peaceable break with amniotic fluid and that their experiences in
pools, oceans, lakes, and rivers all have to do with their perpetually
failed efforts to return to the prenatal self. I am certain, though, that
nothing could be less true. I believe, instead, that swimmers are people who love being born and who want to do it again and again, day
after day, every day.

The Delaware River

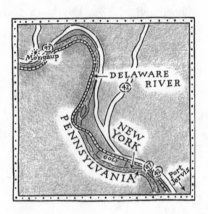

I DON'T KNOW WHAT the word is, but I believe it may exist in some other language. It would be the word for a future tradition, something you do once and know right away that it is something you will repeat time and again. That was how it began with swimming rivers. Thirteen days after our swim across the Hudson River, August 29, 2001, the planes flew into the World Trade Center, and in the months that followed, whenever I glanced at the photograph of the five of us standing at the edge of the river, it seemed to be a small portrait of optimism and oblivion. I had sent a copy of that photograph to Onni where she lives with her family in lower Manhattan. Although I had posted it to her from the Hudson Valley, no more than seventy-five miles north, it took several weeks to reach her, and by the time it did, the envelope I had put it in was smudged with ash. For a long time, the photograph, a little three-by-five image of tenacity and persistence, remained tacked to a bulletin board in their loft. In the face of catastrophe, people often have some sense that they can only move ahead in very small increments; in this case, a picture tacked on the wall and the idea of swimming across another river were two such increments. After that, it has seemed ever more important for both of us to begin each autumn by swimming across a river, some small, personal trial by water that could secure safe passage into the coming year.

So in the late summer of 2002, she and I were determined to go back to the Hudson River. A torrential summer storm prevented us from swimming on the afternoon we had planned, and by the time the skies had finally cleared a day later, the pilot of our escort boat had left for Boston. I looked downriver, then, to other local marinas to see who else could be found to accompany us across the river. My first stop was at the Dutchess Boat Club in Beacon, New York, which I quickly found to be elegant nomenclature for what was little more than a saloon and a launching area for speedboats. Inside the ramshackle white clapboard building, a couple of elderly men were watching a Yankees game, and they met my query about a boat with geniality and enthusiasm, which I soon found was not for our swim but for the sheer entertainment of imagining reasons to disparage it. Cheerily reciting liability concerns and issues of swimmer safety, they cataloged an assortment of legal reasons that would prevent the club from having any association with our swim.

As I left, though, I noticed another low building a couple of hundred feet to the north with a small, hand-painted sign announcing the Beacon Sloop Club. The small building was sheathed in brown shingles in a variety of hues, shapes, and patterns, suggesting that repairs here were an ad hoc affair, and the building itself appeared to be dwarfed by a massive stone chimney. A couple of old buoys hung on its side in a halfhearted effort to be decorative, but its most salient feature was the spruce tree emerging from the roof. Much later I was to hear how the decision had been made when the building had been enlarged to save the obstructing tree by building around it. But even without knowing that, the sight of the roof shingles carefully cut to allow for the tree reflects something about the accommodating attitude with which the denizens of this club view events in the natural world. Later I would also learn that the sloop club was built on what had been a garbage lot during the seventies, a time when Beacon's riverfront was viewed as little more than a place to dump trash; but even today, its persona has no pretensions, as though even the building knows that the elegance and grandeur of the scene lies in the water just beyond. And while I didn't see any sloops moored anywhere near this rundown building, its real estate on the banks of the river couldn't help but give it a sense of dignity. By now any real hope for finding a boat had been replaced by a simple curiosity as to how this club might live up or down to its name. An elderly man repairing the front stoop listened with faint interest as I explained, again, that we were looking for an escort boat to accompany a group of swimmers across the river.

"Let me take you indoors," he said. "There's someone you need to meet." When I followed him into the dark interior of the club, he introduced me to a man who was sweeping the floor with an old broom. It was the singer, songwriter, and veteran environmental activist Pete Seeger, who was trying to spruce up the place. Seeger eyed me up and down, then said, "Swimmers, that's just what I'm looking for."

Wearing old jeans and a red turtleneck sweater, Seeger is a hybrid river rat and Buddhist monk. His charm is in no way compromised by a certain calculating shrewdness. The dusty lounge of the club was clearly a kind of riverside living room to him. He has sailed up and down the Hudson River for over four decades, promoting environmental awareness in general and advocating cleaning up the Hudson in particular. In the late sixties, he had had the idea to raise the money to build the *Clearwater*, a historic replica of an eighteenth-century

Hudson River trade ship, and today the 106-foot wooden sloop is both a symbol of the river's renewal as well as a floating classroom that delivers environmental education and programs. Since it was launched in 1969, the *Clearwater* has given lessons in river ecology to some 450,000 school kids and sponsored riverfront festivals; in 2003 it was named to the National Register of Historic Places. Today it is owned by some eight thousand members of a nonprofit organization that takes on myriad issues, including PCB cleanup of the river, illegal discharging at plants on the river, and innumerable local land-use and development causes.

Seeger loves the river's eddies and currents, its coves and shoreline, and knows them well. And he seems to have acquired an instinctive sense of just how the affairs of the river should run. So when he outlined his plan for me, it was with the clarity and assurance not only of the spiritually certain but of the scientifically correct. "I've been thinking about something for a while," he said. "Here's what I want to do. I'm going to put the boat"—by which I assumed he meant the *Clearwater*—"in the middle of the river. Then we'll have all the swimmers start out at different times, depending on their speed and ability. And then, the idea is that they'll all get to the boat, the finish line, at the same time. Everyone in the race is going to win! They're all going to be equal. Don't you think that's a great idea? There's not nearly enough equality in this world, don't you think?"

Seeger was as gracious as he was persuasive, and he asked me where I lived. "Near LaGrange," I told him, adding needlessly, "It's about twenty or so miles from here." At this his eyes shone and a beatific look came across his face, and he said, "Yes, I was there once, twenty or thirty years ago . . . we may have done a concert there." He spoke of it with nostalgia and longing, as though the town I lived in was some distant province of pleasure that he had once been blessed to visit. "I may go back someday," he said with hope of this apparent Shangri-la that was so close and yet so far. "Come anytime," I felt compelled to say. And I realized then that this is the way it is with

Pete. He has an innate respect for place, and his true wonderment of the Hudson Valley in particular, and of all of sea-to-shining-sea America in general, maybe really any place at all, is intact and undiminished. His allegiance to the Hudson River is legendary, but he's got a broader attentiveness to place, and he believes my little overdeveloped town whose farms have long given way to development, strip malls, video shacks, and pizza huts is worth loving.

Part of the reason Pete Seeger has managed to be as effective as he is is that people find themselves reflexively agreeing to whatever it is he is proposing. What gives the trickster his grace is the conviction that other people, when pointed in the correct direction, will do the right thing. So when he suggested that the Grand Hudson Equality Swim take place in a month, in mid-October during the sloop club's annual Pumpkin Festival, I found myself nodding in agreement, until I realized that the water temperature would surely have a prohibitive chill. It wasn't the first time, I was sure, he had tried to talk a complete stranger into jumping into a cold river if he thought it was something that would better the world. "Well, then," he said, quick to dismiss my reluctance, "next summer, then. In July, for the Strawberry Festival. Or August, the Corn Festival."

I thought about how the *Clearwater* had started with little more than Seeger passing the hat and having a concert, and at that moment, neither the idea of the group swim nor of human equality seemed especially far-fetched. But Seeger's plans notwithstanding, the club had neither a boat nor a captain available for a lesser enterprise in the next few days, and as things turned out, it would be another couple of years before the swim for equality would actually take place. But all that only strengthened our resolve to swim across a river. Which is why Onni and I set our sights on a thinner, lesser river and how we came to the Delaware.

The Delaware River starts in Schoharie County in upstate New York and runs into the Delaware Bay 360 miles to the south. The tidal section begins in Trenton, New Jersey, which is also where the river's identity shifts suddenly and dramatically. The river has been called *bipolar* and *schizophrenic,* anthropomorphic terms that are appropriate because it is human intervention that has constructed the schism. While the upper reaches of the river from its source to Trenton are today pristine wilderness and recreation areas, the 135-mile stretch below Trenton has been given to industry; spills from crude oil transported to the six refineries on that section of the river that supply some 70 percent of gas and heating oil used on the East Coast are not uncommon.

The wilderness writer and river rat Edward Abbey wrote, "I detest the word resource. How could a wild river, part of nature's bloodstream, ever come to be regarded primarily as a damned resource? As if it were no more than a vein of coal, a field of cabbages, a truckload of cow manure?" Abbey, of course, went on to recognize the value of believing the river to be a resource, and though he was talking about western rivers whose waters are routinely contested, diverted, rerouted, and dammed for parched desert landscapes, the Delaware River is a good example of an eastern river in which erratic management strategies have often compromised both the quality of river water and its flow.

Because the Delaware is a boundary for four states—New York, New Jersey, Delaware, and Pennsylvania—its use and management have been routinely contested. Throughout the nineteenth century, deforestation severely altered the watershed. Unpredictable flooding and soil erosion reshaped the riverbed into wider and more shallow channels, while waste from local mills and tanning factories assaulted water quality. A century later, the construction of reservoirs that would supply drinking water for New York City further increased the river's artificial water flow, putting greater stress on the river ecosystem. And as water-flow requirements grew, water use tended to be addressed with little consideration to the river's ecosystem, and fish and insect life suffered from artificial and unpredictable flow.

Not until the formation of the Delaware River Basin Commission in 1961 did the federal government acknowledge the value of regional resource management that could address conflicts about the allocation of drinking water, river pollution, and land use and development along the river. That same year, a formal definition of *water pollution* was determined at an international conference in Geneva, Switzerland, but its imprecise, even gentlemanly phrasing reflects the vagueness with which it was regarded: "Water is considered polluted when its composition or state is directly or indirectly modified by human activity to an extent such that it is less suitable for purposes it could have served in its natural state."

In the mid-seventies, the New York State Department of Environmental Conservation began to address the recreational uses of the river, and at the turn of this century, the Delaware River Foundation was established to promote the stewardship of the upper Delaware river system. Today, the Delaware River Basin Commission is working collaboratively with the foundation, the Nature Conservancy, and other entities to ensure a water management program that recognizes the importance of a balance between ecological, recreational, and economic concerns; and that maintains the river for recreation while continuing to meet the water-supply needs of both river communities and New York City. While the water of the upper Delaware is clean enough to supply New York City with 800 million gallons of water for drinking each day, its headwaters also offer pristine trout streams and waters for canoeing and kayaking.

The spot that Onni and I picked for our swim was just above Port Jervis, New York, where the river still marks the divide between New York and Pennsylvania. While that section of the river is well above the Delaware Water Gap, a spectacular two-mile gorge carved by the river in the Kittatinny Mountains, it has been rehabilitated to resemble its former unspoiled beauty. Bald eagles nest in the stands of trees towering over the river, while its woodlands are habitat for raccoons, beaver, muskrat, and mink. The river here can be fished for trout and smallmouth bass, and in the spring, shad spawn here as well. Route 97 meanders along a ridge above Port Jervis and offers panoramic views of the river snaking its way below between two ridges, before it levels off and follows the riverbank.

I had found myself here the previous January and remembered the river in its winter manifestation. It is easy to believe that the flowing water of a river works as some primal reminder of the flow in our own veins, but there is something in frozen water that reaches us just as deeply; we have an affinity with what is frozen as well as with what is flowing. The river that morning had provided a comprehensive index of ice, water stilled in every way imaginable: great scabs of green ice stalled in their downstream journey; inert hunks of ice that seemed to have been halted in midstream but were, in fact, river rocks encrusted with layer upon layer of crackled blue ice; fragile sheet ice at the river's edge bracketing the current; and on the rocky overhangs along the shore, immense, almost grotesque sculptures of icicles.

Its own little ice museum, the river spoke that morning to all the ways we find ourselves stopped and stilled, all the ways that we can encounter the fact of a small glacier taking up residence in our own veins, all the ways that we can be stunned into our own immobility by coming upon unexpected information, for example, or in confronting the awkward silence that settles in when a relationship has run out of words or when desire has ebbed or been thwarted. I remember the small sense of paralysis that I had felt a year earlier when my doctor had found a lump in my breast. He had made an effort not to be overly concerned, so it wasn't until a couple of days later when I called to make the appointment for a mammogram that the fear settled in. The radiologist had reprimanded me for waiting, then added, "I think you should come in immediately," and the urgency in her tone had stunned me. Although the lump turned out to be nothing worrisome, the dazzling stillness and symmetry of ice crystals that winter morning at the river were some corollary in the natural world to my reaction on hearing her words. It only makes sense that these particles of the river arrested are every bit as familiar to the human consciousness as the image of the green river in its full fluency. Ice clarifies deadlock. Maybe this is why we are so innately drawn to nature—because even in our most unconscious moments, all of its details, all of its minutiae, illuminate us to ourselves.

The river was fluent when Onni had camped there with her husband and sons the year before, and she remembered it as a good place for a swim. Her advice on such matters is to be seriously considered. Like most people of intelligence and imagination, she doesn't hesitate to contradict herself. Born and raised in New York City, she is strictly urban, which has never stopped her from talking often and longingly of living in the country; for someone who has spent her entire adult life on Manhattan Island, she also has compiled a comprehensive interior catalog of tides, currents, and water temperatures of swimming holes around the world. She can speak persuasively of lakes in the Catskill Mountains, waterfalls in Vermont, ponds in upstate New York, rivers in Poland, beaches in Greece, and her intelligence on these matters reminds me of the fact that the more unlikely the source, the more sound the information is bound to be.

As a counselor in the New York City public school system, she has often been tempted to believe that her work accounts for little; the scarce resources allocated to public education and the limited amount of time she is able to spend with her students are small salve to the social ills they come burdened with: poverty, frayed families, learning disabilities, a social system that has failed them. It is an environment in which a complicated network of fiscal, social, political, educational, and emotional needs all feed ceaselessly upon each other. Maybe it is a result of engaging in that kind of unquantifiable work, but when she is swimming in a pond or a pool or a lake, she often sets up a regimen, a fixed ritual of twenty laps or thirty or fifty times across and back. Swimming across rivers especially seems a more measurable task than her work; the width of a river is a finite and calculable distance and offers a sense of resolution that does not come so readily when you are trying to understand the origins of a third grader's depression or when you are trying to explain to an urban teenager why gang members may not make reliable friends. "When I am swimming across a river," she said to me once, "it's something I know I can finish."

Route 97 finally led us down to flat ground again, near the site of the old village of Mongaup at the mouth of the Mongaup River, a tributary to the Delaware. The village is gone today, and in its place is a parking lot for fishermen and boaters. We followed an obscure access path to the river through shrubs and bushes. Remnants of old stone walls and foundations and an overgrown gully alluded to the canal and towpath that had once run parallel to the river. Mills and small factories on the upper Delaware had once made it a place of purpose and industry, but it seemed now to be a landscape of recreation.

Or so it seemed. Without warning, then, the path and then the calm of the afternoon were bisected by a gently rippling length of black cable. People claim fear of heights, public speaking, flying in airplanes, but I have always claimed snakes as my agent of terror. Fear and reason are natural adversaries, and the sight of even the thinnest green grass snake can send me into a panic. But this was a different animal. A black rat snake, some five feet long, and its midsection a diameter of five inches, was ever so slowly, gently, and, to my mind, with utmost malevolence making its circuit across our path. Suddenly a deep current of fear insinuated itself into this narrow river.

My own terror of snakes has prohibited me on occasion from going into basements, entering doorways, stepping over logs and stone walls. But a different logic presented itself now. There was something so incongruous about this oily black cable slowly twisting itself across the sunny afternoon that any sensible person could only consider it a grotesque apparition, some unreal visitation that exists only in the imagination. Besides, so unexpected and monstrous was this particular snake that the likelihood of encountering it, or anything like it, again in a single afternoon seemed impossible. I don't know that such laws of probability are relevant on the banks of the Delaware River, but it was enough to allow me to stick with the plan of swimming in this river. A more relevant logic might simply have been that, despite all appearances, such snakes are relatively harmless. But that is not what kept me going; with a fear that was deeply entrenched, I simply went ahead believing that I was unlikely to encounter the same bad luck twice in a single day. Sometimes any logic, not necessarily correct logic, is enough to get you through a moment of panic. Apparent sense, rather than sense itself, is sometimes enough.

Besides, Onni was enrapt. As an actor for many years with the La Mama Repertory Company in New York, she has performed in numerous productions of classical Greek theater. Her work in two different productions of *Electra* had required that she handle the first time a python, the second time time a boa constrictor. She had been willing, eager even, both times, and both times she had been bitten. I knew all of this, and yet her calm indifference to the rat snake astounded me, and when I could no longer escape the fact that she might even have taken some delight in its appearance, I became a little annoyed. Another's indifference toward one's own fears is inevitably belittling, and for a moment I could scarcely believe we were occupying the same spot of grass on the same afternoon, and only grudgingly did I come to accept the fact that one objective of traveling with another person is to have them there to do exactly that—disparage and otherwise diminish your fears. Although that afternoon we had not yet made any specific plans to go from one river to another and another, looking back on it, I can see it was not only twenty-five years of friendship that caused us to be compatible traveling partners, but her utter disregard for those things that make me apprehensive; or maybe I just saw her as fearless.

I considered myself fortunate simply to have had just a visual encounter with the rat snake. In *The Blue Nile*, Alan Moorehead speaks of an explorer in the twenties who, scrambling down a ledge of rock as he was investigating a waterfall, reached out to grab for a branch, and found himself clinging to the tail of a python. He survived the episode, we are told, but I cannot imagine how. Still, it occurs to me that in the single instant between grabbing the python and realizing what it was he was clinging to, he found just time enough to get the necessary support and stability. It is, after all, an ordinary human reaction in times of trouble to reach out and grab exactly the wrong thing—a drink, a cigarette, or the person who *cannot* be counted upon—and nonetheless get some degree of comfort only because we believe we are getting it. Whether it is reaching for the wheel of the car when it should have been the telephone or a glass of wine when it might have been a sheet of stationery, an envelope, stamp, I know I have grabbed the tail of that python myself on occasion.

Moorehead says that of those early explorers in the eighteenth century, there were two types: romantics, sophisticates who assumed the costumes and the habitats of the people they traveled among, believing they could somehow be counted as natives among them; and the more practical men who made no pretense of such assimilations, instead asserting their own identities with a kind of pride and efficiency. Grabbing the tail of a python, it seems to me, would be enough to turn instantaneously a man with the character of the former to one of the latter.

And so we walked another ten or fifteen feet to a sandy scrap of beach at the edge of the river. Swimming in the upper Delaware is an activity laced with ambiguity. We had already passed a sign warning us that there was ABSOLUTELY NO SWIMMING IN THE DELAWARE RIVER. But I already knew that. A phone call earlier in the week to the office of the Upper Delaware Scenic and Recreational River had alerted me to the fact that none of the public accesses on either the New York or Pennsylvania side of the river permitted swimming. While there was no question as to the water's cleanliness, its fast currents, unpredictable water levels, class I and II rapids, rocks, submerged debris, and sudden drop-offs all made swimming there dangerous in the eyes of the various organizational agencies managing river use. "There's no public swimming," I was told. The ranger then added, "That doesn't mean you can't swim in the river."

I am by now familiar with—and often charmed by—these odd and overtly contradictory directives that seem inevitable during the course of travel anywhere. As a teenager I once took a train down the Nile Valley with my sister, and we were instructed to stop in a small village for a permit to visit the temples at Luxor. No permits were being issued that day, the official told us as he lazily swatted at flies. A ceiling fan rotating casually over our heads did nothing to assuage the oppressive desert heat, which, along with our inability to speak Arabic and our fatigue caused us to slouch silently and sullenly on a bench as we considered what to do. We waited. And waited. An hour or so later, the same man opened a file on his desk, took out the necessary papers, stamped them, and handed them to us without explanation. A homeless man in a New York subway station once told me with somber certainty the trains had stopped running that afternoon, just moments before a train rumbled into the station. Driving to a furniture warehouse in the Bronx, once, I stopped for directions, and halfway through labored instructions involving expressways, U-turns, and a highway underpass, I happened to look up and see the sign for the warehouse. It was half a block away.

Much has been made in recent years of the manner in which people ask for directions: Women do, men don't; women admit to feeling lost, while men are unlikely to feel lost. But of infinitely greater interest to me is the way people give directions. I don't know why it is, but people, especially those in some temporary position of self-appointed authority, are drawn to giving confusing, self-contradictory, and otherwise baffling advice. Maybe it is the trickster in all of us. Maybe it is just some universal law of human communication to create mystery where there is none; as though our own intentions and desires don't make our travels on this earth circuitous enough, strangers, when asked, are often compelled to complicate them further. In this instance, I was simply told not to swim at a public access. If I could, however, take myself to some area of the river not open to the public, I might consider swimming. But not without a PFD, a personal flotation device.

Before we even considered our own swim, though, we took in the host of other activities on the Delaware River. The place where any two rivers meet tends to be a place of industry. Here, where the Mongaup River meets the Delaware, two locks had been constructed in the early nineteenth century. In the late 1820s, the Delaware and Hudson Canal had been built to transport anthracite coal from the mines of northeastern Pennsylvania to the Hudson Valley, where it was then shipped to New England and New York City. Until the end of that century, when railroads became the more efficient means of transport and the canals were drained, this spot on the river had been home to a store, telegraph office, schoolhouse, boatyard, and houses, along with a feeder dam that had been built to divert water into the canal. Of these, little remain today; there are vestiges of stonework from the locks and towpath and only the outline of the canal, a dry trough in the earth filled with leaves, all spectral reminders of the river's previous activity. Which is not to say the convergence of the two rivers is lacking in industry now, but that the business of coal and canals was replaced by the commerce of recreation.

The blazing September day was more like midsummer than early autumn, and while the river may not have been open to swimmers, it was a shimmering, reflective stage for all other manners of water activity which we watched from our bit of beach. Immediately downstream an enormous vessel had parked itself. *Pontoon boat* seemed inadequate terminology for the immense rubber raft floating on pontoons, large enough to carry fourteen people and a dog, a twenty-first-century equivalent of Hogarth's merry debauchers. They had with them vast coolers, a keg of beer, a tape deck, tubes, and floats, a jolly carnival of rafters outfitted for every kind of pleasure that might be had on the Delaware River in late summer. Sports technology is usually about efficiency and about how new composite materials and technotextiles that look to NASA or the military for their design genesis allow people to go farther, higher, faster, longer. But this lumbering, awkward float had made its own sport of all that, adapting the expedience of military design for nothing more than the pursuit of pure, indulgent folly.

Just upstream, where the water is more peaceable, was a different theater of indolence: Installing themselves within pods of inner tubes, floaters of all ages and sizes were drifting lazily down the river like a fleet of human-industrial mutants, proving that sports and somnambulation can be congenial partners. Tubing, a near effortless way to experience the river, is an exercise that commands little respect. Perhaps it is because the equipment itself is so primitive or because tubing requires minimal talent or expertise; there is no way to steer or stop the thing other than using one's own limbs, and an old inner tube doesn't follow any given direction except that of the river. Small wonder that in a culture that puts a high value on action, knowledge, and a sense of purpose, tubing is generally regarded as the lowest form of river recreation, the dumb cousin to kayaking and canoeing, which require grace, skill, agile maneuvers of all sorts. Surely, though, the pleasures of drifting downstream in an inner tube should not be so easily dismissed. If a river can appear idle and lazy, why not follow its example? The seventeenth-century Japanese poet Basho wrote of his travels as a meditative experience; floating downriver was occasion for reflection, and it seems to me that given the choice, Basho might easily have selected an inflated inner tube to drift down the river in a shiftless fashion over a more purposeful superlight polyethylene kayak or a fiberglas canoe.

Things were busier on our little spot on the river. The lusty festival of the Hogarth revelers had drifted downstream, replaced by more austere river runners. Where the two rivers meet, a series of boulders had created rapids, a challenge to boaters, and we watched a battalion of red canoes that had just successfully navigated the rapids pass us with a certain triumphant calm. Shortly afterward, a flotilla of kayakers swept by in a beautifully choreographed water ballet. Others that followed were more athletic. Wearing canary yellow neoprene bodysuits with stripes and checks, the kayakers appeared as some exotic river species of their own, catapulting themselves through the rapids, then into the deeper channel, capsizing their little vessels at will, then righting them again, demonstrating with balletic grace a whole index of aquatic catastrophe. Kayaking gear flaunts a particular eccentricity of color and form: thin rubber shoes with sticky rubber soles and mesh panels for drainage, carbon fiber paddles with rubber grips wielded like some strange antennae, nylon flotation vests in brilliant greens and reds that conform to the body like the shell of some tropical rodent. And then there are the kayaks themselves, superlight polyethylene vessels that seem to ride the water with an intent and desire of their own. And their pantomime, a miniature circus that made a parody of all water disaster, came out right every time. And so it went throughout the afternoon.

Contemporary philosophers and social critics often point out that our appreciation of the natural world today may be contingent upon how we make it manageable and accessible; and that artificial interventions may be essential to the pleasure we take in nature. As I watched the assorted activities on the Delaware, it was hard to avoid the thought that they were their own form of colonization. While the human intervention on this upper stretch of the river seemed remote from the industry that defined the river downstream, it nonetheless reflected the human imagination at work in a different way.

In an essay called "The Dilemma of Wilderness," the biologist David Graber writes that today wilderness has acquired a mythology that reflects values particular to our time. "It now functions to provide solitude and counterpoint to technological society in a landscape that is managed to reveal as few traces of the passage of other humans as possible. Contemporary wilderness visitors are just that. Unlike the hunters and gatherers who preceded them on the land, moderns who enter wilderness do so not to live on the land, nor to use it, but rather to experience it spiritually. The ecosystem is defined on its own terms, but this wilderness is a social construct." Watching the canoers and the kayakers that afternoon, and certainly considering our own endeavor, I realized how often we find that comfort in the natural world has to do with how we domesticate it.

Romantics or practical men—I wonder which category Moorehead would place the kayakers in. Surely their gear, their superlight poly-ethylene kayaks and nylon flotation vests, serves as evidence of their practical concerns, their ruggedness, their preparedness for all of nature's uncertainties. But it seems to me that some part of their travels downstream are informed as well by a sense of romance. Any of us who look to the natural world for respite are indulging as well in an inevitable sense of escapism. I would imagine that since the time of the travels Moorehead was writing about, the world has changed in a way that allows us—indeed demands of us—that we accommodate both personas; river travel is equal parts efficiency and escapism.

While we were far from alone on the river that afternoon, because we were without any such vessels ourselves, we were on a very different trajectory. As our intention was to go across the river, rather than down it, our difference in purpose seemed to situate us on a different part of the river. Not to mention the fact that we were going to be in, rather than on, the water. "Like any honest riverman, I detest getting wet," Edward Abbey once said, and there does seem to exist some unspoken rule among river runners that being in the water is to be avoided; and that, kayakers' theatrics aside, the skill and grace of running a river have to do with staying dry.

I wouldn't argue with that logic. To have an expertise in anything may require a small distance. My father was a journalist, and when he wrote profiles, he made it a practice never to interview his subjects directly. Friends, family, teachers, colleagues might all be spoken with at length, and almost always an accurate and revealing profile emerged. I would suppose it's true that knowledge, whether it is of a river or a person, may come from establishing this small distance and the perspective it allows. But I would be the first to admit that it is not really knowledge I am after. Immersion is about something else, and so somewhere in a lull between the rafters, kayakers, canoers, we took our own swim.

We had not thought to come equipped with personal flotation devices; what we did have, though, were matching bathing suits. Earlier in the day we had stopped at Swimwear Anywhere, an outlet catering to tourists, and for five dollars apiece we had each bought a nylon bathing suit cut for lap swimming and printed with a loud geometric pattern of turquoise, aqua, and cerulean blue the garishness of which seems a characteristic of so much sports attire. We had decided these would be our official team suits, though what the team or its goals might be were yet undecided. Of no matter. It is not unheard of to look to one's accessories for clarification—of motive, goal, direction. Besides, standing on the riverbank in those matching suits, we could entertain the illusion of authenticity; it might not be exactly what you would call a seriousness of purpose, but I felt certain those matching suits conferred upon us some degree of proficiency or compatibility, even, with the neoprene-attired kayakers.

Stepping across stones that were slick with moss and into the current, I wondered whether this was the kind of danger that was bright and easy and sweet or if I had just imagined some sense of menace, but then we were in the water, and the apprehension vanished. The river was wide and shallow here, a product of generations of deforestation that increased the water runoff into the river and allowed for the accumulation of silt in the riverbed. It is hard to imagine that the river was reshaped, the contours of its banks reconfigured, the depth of its bed revised and reformed, all simply as an incidental result of deforestation. You might think that an act so grand as reshaping a river might require forethought and deliberation, or at least some kind of purposeful work, but like so many of our worst acts, it doesn't take intent; it only requires thoughtlessness.

Although that section of the river wasn't much more than fifty yards wide, it had unexpected pockets of deep water only a few feet from the shore, and those, along with the strength of current, came on suddenly. While the water of the Hudson had a sweetness redolent of the tides where the river finally empties, this water introduced itself by way of its origins. Flowing from the mountains, it came with a crispness, a purity, a cleanness. There was even a clarity to its taste, and if water can taste fast, this did that too. And while the slight chill in the water suggested its source in the mountains, it was also threaded with the chill of the coming months, and its current seemed to lead not only downstream but into the coolness of the new season.

As the kayakers' aquatic exercises had demonstrated, this section of the river is quick and its sequence of pools and eddies unpredictable. Although it was late summer by then, and the river was low, there were several unexpectedly deep pools midriver. Immersed in the swift current, then, I was grateful to find, from time to time, a submerged rock which offered a foothold or a crevice to grab on to. Invisible from the shore, these occasional and unexpected supports slowed the passage and afforded some measure of control. As narrow as the river was, I found myself in one of those situations in which you are unable to gauge the intensity of experience until you search out a stable point of reference that is a substantial distance from your current position, when experience cannot be fully assimilated until you fix upon something outside of it, which in this case happened to be a rock on the opposite side. It makes sense to me how the word *current* refers to both the direction and pull of the water and being in and of the moment, because those two different meanings converged that afternoon in the river. I found myself swept by a large gray rock that only moments earlier had seemed to be far downstream. Of course it was not the current itself that signaled to me to its own strength and speed, but the stone remnants of a bridge abutment, a towering elm tree, a rotting log, all of them fixed immobile on the opposite bank, and all of them slowly receding behind me.

There are times we all want to be swept away; there are times we all *need* to be swept away. Maybe the trick lies in having some say over what it is that so sweeps you, having some small piece of determination, participating in the choice if it is at all possible. Often it is not. My family and my house are my ballast, I know, and the structure and order of ordinary domestic life ground me in every way possible. I am not so foolish as to disregard the fact that setting the table, making a salad, pouring the wine are the quotidian tasks that braid a sense of order into my life. And if there are times when I look to be swept away from all of this, insofar as I have the good fortune to have any say in the matter, those few minutes in the Delaware River on a sunny September morning seem the sound choice. If I have any aspiration to be a contemporary wilderness visitor, it is to make that choice from time to time. Those few minutes in the Delaware came and went quickly. Just as quickly and as unexpectedly the current calmed. No more than ten or twelve minutes had passed, and we were swimming in a more leisurely way to the other side.

Swimming back across, we knew what to expect. If the warning signs had fostered a sense of uncertainty about getting in the river, by now we had made its aquaintance. How quickly any kind of apprehension can be made to vanish with just the smallest amount of information! We humans seem hardwired to know that whether it's food or words or love or knowledge, a little goes a long way. We don't need much. Getting by requires only a sparse vocabulary. Onni and I had only a few facts: where the riverbed dropped off and where we could safely step on it again; where the current quickened and where it would quiet again; where to find a rock that might offer a foothold and where there was a slippery slab of gray granite. Its flat face just beneath the surface of the water was a good place to sit midstream and watch the river as it ran all around us. And that was enough for our doubt to drift downstream.

"Life consists with wildness," said Henry David Thoreau. "The most alive is the wildest." And I am certain this has not to do with some ability to set up camp in the woods or build a fire or traverse some icy rock face, but rather with a willingness to entertain those thoughts that lie outside the sphere of personal experience. Maybe what we are really looking for when we turn to nature is not so much a river's torrents or a mountain's icy peak, but instead, the ability to think and imagine outside the confines of our own biases and pre-conceptions, the capacity to feel passion or devotion or sympathy to-ward something or someone or someplace that may not warrant it. Or even to lose your heart instantaneously or to find unexpected truth in the words of an adversary. It is the capacity for recognizing the land-scape of uncertainty within ourselves, that rugged topography that comes with unpredictable thought and feeling. Caught in the rush of the current, I imagined this to be possible.

On our way back, Onni saw a twenty-dollar bill underwater. We didn't pause to examine how this could possibly be, and besides, the reptile vision of just a few hours ago had made me receptive to the notion of startling and unexpected apparitions. So instead, we just looked for it for a while, in the crevices of rocks, under rotting branches, and along the stones of the riverbed. It could have been a leaf or a shard of light reflected in the water; it also might have been some visual pun, one of those small optical pranks the human brain sometimes plays in which the river current for an instant had been visually translated as monetary currency. She told me later, "There is some kind of hole there," and I didn't ask whether she meant in the river or in her life. "I don't know why I didn't just reach out and take it. Or why I couldn't find it later."

There are divers in the Philippines who can descend two hundred feet into the sea to pluck pearls off the ocean floor; and there are chil-dren in Thailand who are able to forage for sea cucumbers and tiny shellfish underwater that remain invisible to others. There are scien-tific explanations for this that have to do with the density of water; because it is similar to that of the eye's fluids, the refractive power of the eye's corneal surface is diminished underwater. Yet it remains possible, it seems, for some people to physically reshape the eye's lens so that both the refraction of light and the ability to see underwater are enhanced. But I also know that when one is submerged in water, there is often little difference between what the eye fixes upon and what it supposes. Under the surface of the water, we are all given to imagining.

In Amazonian folklore, Encanto is an enchanted subaquatic world full of riches and magic, and the Encantados who occupy that world take to giving human visitors valuable prizes and riches. There are accounts of houses constructed of silver and gemstones, hammocks woven with threads of gold, a river floor that radiates with light, and visitors who happen to stumble upon this realm that is both remote and close at hand are said to undergo some sort of transformation, spiritual, physical, or sexual. The anthropologist Candace Slater documents the elusiveness of the river kingdom as a place where the usual fixed boundaries between human and nonhuman, earth and water, life and death become blurred. Perhaps my swimming partner is attuned to these visions of extravagance in the underwater world. No doubt, underwater, the boundaries between the real and the imagined can blur; reality and desire are natural confederates. It is a borderless landscape that speaks to our appetite for the unfathomable. And as much as we try to colonize what is wild in the river so that it can accommodate us comfortably, there remains something unfamiliar and strange in the underwater realm. I identify myself as a swimmer, a writer, a parent, I think of myself as all of these things, yet if I am also in part what David Graber calls a contemporary wilderness visitor, it is because a part of me counts on meeting up with that realm of the unknown that inevitably accosts you when you are underwater.

In the end, it didn't matter that we didn't find the twenty-dollar bill, because I thought of Pete Seeger, his vision of equality made manifest on the Hudson River, and how that could be its own parallel river kingdom, a different Encanto ablaze with its own extravagance of hope and vision. I thought of the kayakers' theater of river calamities that managed to right themselves time and again, and I thought of the snake and the fact that there are times in life when even the most deeply flawed logic can triumph over fear, and I thought maybe she had just dreamed that twenty-dollar bill floating downstream. It made sense to me, because it was clear by then that getting across the Delaware River and back had offered us both its own full compensation.

The Connecticut River

My mother grew up in Greenfield, Massachusetts, near the Connecticut River. When my sister and I were children, we would drive across it often when visiting our grandparents, and every time we did that, my mother would inevitably say, "Girls, look, there's the Connecticut River. It's the most beautiful river on earth." She had traveled around the world a number of times. She had lived in Bangkok, a city of small rivers where one can buy everything from mangoes to sapphires in the little boats lining the canals, and in Japan, where running water resonates with spiritual meaning and there is a reverence for all of nature. Still, the Connecticut River remained her ideal of beauty.

And it is a beautiful river, wide and calm, flanked by the willow

43

trees that thrive at water's edge, their delicate branches bracketing the river with a soft frame, and beyond that, rolling woodlands of white oak, sugar maple, yellow birch, and hickory. Part of its beauty has to do with its natural protection. The same shifting black silt that has allowed this lush growth along its banks has made the river difficult to navigate its 410-mile course: The river begins in a series of thin tributaries in northern New Hampshire and ends in the Long Island Sound near Old Lyme, Connecticut, where the Saybrook Sandbar, formed by a natural wash of river sediment, has prohibited it from ever serving as a port. In colonial times, the river was thought to be entirely unnavigable: When the British army invaded the Essex Harbor at the mouth of the river in 1814, soldiers were forced to row up the river in smaller boats to burn the colonists' ships.

Onni and I came to the river by way of Hadley, in western Massachusetts, a river town in every sense of the word. Situated on a peninsula at an especially circuitous bend along the river, the town is bordered on the north, west, and south by the river. The river *defines* it. A broad common, a mile long, 333 feet wide, said to be the longest village green in New England, runs across the peninsula from north to south, with both ends terminating at the river. The north end of the common arrives at a dyke, and since I had first seen this spot six months earlier, I had been drawn to the idea of starting our swim at this end of the Hadley Green.

The Hadley Common serves as a timeline of sorts. The town was first settled in 1659 on the eastern bank of the river as a farming community, which it continued to be until the late nineteenth century. Today, it is a typical twenty-first-century New England hybrid. The white clapboard congregational church, with its antique sixteen-over-sixteen windows, and brick civic buildings have been carefully preserved, and an old barn built in 1782 was moved into the center of town and restored to serve as a farm museum; its exhibits of old plows, threshing and winnowing machines, oxen yokes and harnesses all attest to the region's agricultural past. Yet nearby are insurance offices, the DoNut Man, a Cumberland Farms, all making for a sense of disconnect common to so many old New England towns. The architecture of business from some four centuries has resulted in an uncomfortable convergence of antique heritage and modern convenience that few American town planners have managed to master.

The common, once meant to serve as the communal hub of the village, documents that disconnect. Its residences, farm buildings, and taverns were all built in the seventeenth century as places for people to gather, for animals to graze, for the militia to hold its drills. Surrounding the green, and further defining its function, was an eight-foot-high wall of logs, a palisade, to protect it and the houses lining its perimeter. Today, though, the houses that line the green are a medley of traditional center-hall clapboard townhouses, Cape Cod cottages, a raised ranch—a catalog of eclectic American domestic architecture. It is a fragmented place, and on this August morning, the green itself was empty. There was nothing common on the common ground, as though the very idea of American community life had become extinct. Certainly you couldn't call a place so resonant with historical meaning a dead place, but it was an empty space, and it reminded me of the similarly vacant courtyards at my sons' high school in the Hudson Valley. The layout of classrooms, library, cafeterias, and gym revolves around a system of courtyards that bring light into indoor space. Although there is access to the courtyards themselves, of the many times over the years I have visited the school, never once have I seen students or teachers using them as the congenial outdoor public gathering place they were intended to be.

But if the form and layout of our public places has changed, our need for them appears to be constant. The public function of the Hadley Common has been replaced by a more fluid arena for communal activity more suited to the twenty-first century. Perpendicular to the green was a long dyke running above the river, and joggers used it as a running path; an elderly couple was walking their dog down it, and a woman was picking a bouquet of Queen Anne's lace and goldenrod; as she passed, she sighed and said to no one in particular, "My flower garden had nothing for me this weekend." Below was the theater of the river itself: a kayaker, a couple of teenagers on Jet Skis, a powerboat cruising upstream, and a group of kids playing on a scrap of silt on the other side. The two bands of green were not quite, but almost, converging, one of them static, earthen, still, the other transparent, reflective, fluid. George Santayana once observed that beauty is pleasure objectified, and if it is true that beauty lies in some part in the ability to confer joy, surely the river met such a standard that morning.

Six months earlier, on a wet, gray March afternoon, the river had been swollen from a spring of constant and torrential rain, and looking down on it from the dyke, I couldn't help but feel grateful for the protective sense of height and distance. The rain clouds and the river had seemed engaged in some monumental watery collusion, or perhaps some kind of rivalry about the nature of water and its force. On the day of our swim, though, it was a more placid, reflective landscape. There is nothing grand about the Connecticut River; its function as the mainstream of New England life is generally fulfilled with serene assurance rather than dramatic gestures. Writing about the river in 1907, Edwin M. Bacon noted that "the predominant view of the river is sweet and winsome, rather than proud and majestic. It has its grand moods, but these are brilliant flashes which serve to enhance the exquisiteness of its gentler mien. The Valley's charm is found in the frequency and magnitude of the fertile meadows." His words remain true today, and in the golden sheen of an August morning, the river followed its course with a sense of quietude.

But it did so elusively. By late summer, the lower bank of the dyke had been transformed into a thicket of sumac, jewelweed, clover, ivy, cornflowers, blackberry bushes, goldenrod, a typical New England improvisational hedge of weeds and brambles that was as extravagant as it was impenetrable. River access was no longer possible. It was no longer the surge of the current or the temperature of the water that was prohibitive, but the path to it. In an odd reversal of conditions that the cycles of nature use so frequently to deceive us, the river itself was no longer formidable; it was simply impossible to reach.

A woman walking her dog directed us to a small scrap of dark, silty beach a mile and a half north of Hadley, so we drove north out of town until we saw what looked to be a trail. We parked the car and walked toward the river through woods and a cornfield on a dusty path that might have once been a cow path, but was now a minimally maintained access route for the power lines that cross the river here. And suddenly we stood at the river's edge. In the late seventeenth century, the path had served as transit for a different kind of energy; a ferry had crossed the river at this site, carrying villagers from the west side of the river to the church in the village proper. Now, three centuries later, it was another Sunday morning, and while I knew I didn't share the sense of purpose, faith, or devotion of my predecessors, something, maybe nothing more than the universal quest for community and continuity, allowed me to feel some fleeting kinship with them as I walked out into the river.

For ten feet, then twenty and thirty, the river was barely more than knee-high, and we waded halfway across it, step by step, our disbelief growing in equal measure to our diminishing expectations. I had known that the geography of the Connecticut River was inconsistent, but had little expected that we would be walking across the better part of it. The entire Connecticut River valley was once covered in a sheet of glacial ice a mile thick that began to melt and recede some twenty thousand years ago, eventually forming a lake some two hundred miles long, and that lake receding finally into a river. The accumulation of sediment made for the fertile agricultural soil found in the valley today, and since colonial days, Connecticut Valley farmers have cultivated potatos, onions, grains, corn, wheat, flax, hemp, and tobacco leaves. That same fine soil that had made the river valley such rich farmland over the centuries also makes for morphing sandbars and a constantly shifting channel. Throughout the eighteenth century, before charts were drawn to map the river channel or buoys and markers put out to mark the sandbars, navigation on the river was slow and difficult. Periodically, the twenty-foot channel has to be dredged to accommodate river traffic, and despite that, the passage of anything beyond shallow-draft boats and barges is generally prohibited.

After we had waded out about fifty feet, without warning, the riverbed dropped away. Suddenly the water was deep enough to swim across to the west bank. Swimming across the Connecticut River here was not a matter of miles and hours, but of feet and minutes. Above was another dyke, and beyond that, an expanse of tobacco fields. And even only a foot or two from the bank, the floor of the river was too deep to stand on. A powerboat cruising upriver seemed to come perilously close to the bank, but its operator clearly knew what we were just discovering; at this particular moment in time, the channel hugged the western bank of the river. The river's varying depth is a constant reminder of its unpredictability, its hidden character surely a component in its beauty.

And then, rather than swim back to the point where we had started, we decided instead to swim downstream, eventually finding ourselves drifting down the east bank of the river. The water again became deep, and the course of the deeper channel continued to shift unpredictably down the river for our mile-and-a-half swim. Where shallow, the light played on the rocks on the riverbed; only a foot or two beyond, the water would return to an opaque black. The depth was never where it was anticipated. The fine silt defined our swim in other ways too. Even where the channel was deep, the slightest movement or stroke seemed to stir up the sediment, giving the water an unexpected texture. The river water had what was almost a graininess, and swimming through it was similar to the experience of being tangled up in an ocean wave and to emerge with the sensation that sand had lodged in every pore and crevice of your body. The grit was such that you could taste it, and it gave the water an unexpected sense of materiality. Even several hours after we left the river, a thin film of silt lingered on my skin. The river had attached itself to me.

While our own encounters with the shifting depth and shallows of the river were minor, the placid Connecticut River is capable of much greater deceptions. In 1996, Ed Klekowski, a professor of biology at the University of Massachusetts, and a group of students were routinely tracking the riverbed near the town of Gill, Massachusetts, when their sonar depth sounder detected a large hole some twenty feet beneath the surface, an abyss, some 30 feet wide and 120 feet deep. What they found on subsequent dives must have appeared to be some natural corollary to a chamber in the Dali Museum, its collection of the surreal including freshwater sponges the size of dinner plates and yellow invertebrate blobs that resembled coral along with the preindustrial tools, antique bottles, and bits of collapsed bridges elsewhere on the riverbed. Aside from offering the scientists a vast ecosystem for the study of new animal and plant species, the sheer cliff proved to be a timeline of the valley, with each descending foot reaching back farther into time. In a short film, *Beneath the River,* Klekowski documents the underwater landscape investigated subsequently by divers in this historical archive: At 30 feet, one encounters simply an eerie blackness, a landscape of sensory deprivation; at 90 feet, one finds Mesozoic rocks with the footprints of dinosaurs; and at 120 feet, the time travel takes divers back some 200 million years to the time when the valley was created. While the river appears to follow its course with a sense of calm assurance, its ever-shifting floor suggests that it has a drama but one that is simply unseen.

It is presumed that the abyss was formed some 200 million years ago. Three hundred million years ago, a collision of landmasses—North America, Africa, Eurasia, and Avalonia—formed the supercontinent of Pangaea. When that landmass began to break up 100 million years later and the continents attempted to separate, a variety of fault lines formed, and the Connecticut River marks one of these early fault lines; most of these later aborted, except, of course, the one that is today the eastern seaboard of the United States. (Klekowski explains it by comparing it to the way a pudding cracks; various smaller rifts appear before the real and final break occurs.) A piece of Avalonia, however, remained affixed to North America, at what is now Massachusetts and Connecticut, with the remainder staying with the African landmass. Referring to that geologic occurrence, one woman I know wistfully noted that, improbably though not altogether incorrectly, the quaint Connecticut town she lived in had once in fact been part of the African continent. Or as Klekowski said to me, "Boston ought to be in Libya."

That the land that lies to the east of the river was once part of the landmass that is now Africa seems curious, but such seismic shifts are common in the imagination, a place where landscapes are easily realigned, geography easily reordered, continents of memory easily demolished and remade. Possibly owing to their own character of meandering continuity and irregular currents, rivers all lend themselves to being reconfigured and reimagined. And with its shifting sands and ever-migrating channel, the Connecticut River offers evidence of the idea that nothing is so constant as change itself.

I remember once seeing a drawing by Saul Steinberg, an artist famed for his maps of fantastic landscapes and perspectives. This particular map appeared to chart the waterway of his own life as it meandered across a vast green plain under a milky pink sky. There were a few trees along the river, but no buildings. There were many cities, however, and those included Rome, Roxbury, Wellfleet, Rochester, and Paris, along with many others. Cities had been realigned as they so often are in memory and imagination; Santo Domingo was across the river from Moab, Nice across from Anchorage. And there, across from Kyoto, was Nigeria. My guess is that Steinberg was indulging in that geographic reordering we are so often inclined toward when we think about the events of our lives and the places they occurred; we devise a diagram of different proximities to chart the geography of personal experience.

Yet as improbable as Steinburg's waterway seems, in *A Short History of Nearly Everything* Bill Bryson explains the shifting of the earth's tectonic plates as a somewhat similar process: "The connection between modern landmasses and those of the past were found to be infinitely more complex than anyone had imagined. Kazakstan, it turns out, was once attached to Norway and New England. One corner of Staten Island, but only a corner, is European. So is part of Newfoundland. Pick up a pebble from a Massachusetts beach, and its nearest kin will now be in Africa. The Scottish Highlands and much of Scandinavia are substantially American. Some of the Shackleton Range of Antarctica, it is thought, may once have belonged to the Appalachians of the Eastern U.S. Rocks, in short, get around."

Here, it seems, is one of those splendid occasions on which artist and scientist together arrive, through vastly different paths, at the like conclusion, which is that the earth we live on is capable of grand and inexplicable shifts; and that the rearrangements of its plates is in the natural course of events. Such tectonic realignments give us a logic for those times we feel strange and disoriented on familiar ground, and at the same time, they offer us the possibility of finding familiarity in foreign places. Besides all that, the knowledge that the earth's plates are ever shifting makes me believe that anything is possible, that the sea changes in my own life are a part of the natural course of things. It is proof offered by the physical facts of rock, dirt, and water that the seismic reconfiguration of things can be accommodated, the way, for instance, a relationship between two people can be wrenched apart, then find a way to right itself again, its topography irrevocably changed, its bedrock cracked, shifted, reconfigured, then reattached in some essential way that is, in the end, solid.

We swam downstream, a mile or more. Or perhaps we didn't swim so much as drift. The Connecticut River is known as a *soft-water river*, a term that refers to the chemistry of the water, which is low in total ion concentration and circumneutral, or with pH that is less acidic. But the term seems to capture its character in a more general way too, speaking to its gentle bends and easy current. The river has been accused of loitering more than flowing. This is not a river that sweeps you away, but one that takes you gently by the hand and says with quiet assurance, "This way now." Tendrils clung to my feet, then seemed to disentwine themselves, and the visibility underwater came and went, but mostly went. This was beauty without clarity. And this is the secret beauty of swimming; it is one of those sports that can be practiced with something close to indolence. It is not about speed or distance or progress. Certainly it can be about these things. Designers and engineers working on something called *computational fluid dynamic analyses* have researched ways in which the human body can move through water most efficiently, and each year manufacturers introduce new gear to enable swimmers to go farther faster, swimsuits accessorized with "riblets" fashioned after the grooves used on airplane fuselage and strapless goggles that are said to reduce drag.

I imagine swimming through water wearing such gear. Would a nylon suit with riblets have somehow further reduced the distance between me and the current? Or strapless goggles have somehow streamlined my underwater vision? The beauty of swimming is that such efficiency need not be observed at all. One can swim languidly and slowly; swimming is one of the few human endeavors in which activity and idleness can coincide, and it is entirely possible, often even desirable, to be a lazy swimmer. I am certain that there is something about exercising regular strokes that reaffirms the human appreciation of rhythm. We live in a world in which we are increasingly distanced from the natural rhythm of things. Our diet usually has little to do with what foods are in season; when the days are short, we simply turn on the lights earlier; and while our travels may be inconvenienced by climate, certainly they are not governed by it. I can't help but wonder, then, if part of the appeal of swimming simply has to do with the reaffirmation of the body in a simple rhythm.

Continuity is in the character of any river, and what a river does best is just go on and on and on. And it invites you to extend yourself in the same way. With the possible exception of the wind, a river is that feature of the natural landscape that knows best how to reach; of course a continuing stretch of river is called a *reach*. And when you find yourself immersed in that, the possibilities for nearly anything seem as though they could go on and on as far as the eye can see. All along the way, we passed little scrabbly paths, tiny strips of beach, a decaying dock, a set of rotting steps, and thirty feet later, a more recently built pier floating on four bright blue barrels, then an old inner tube tied to a tree. Each was its own interlude in the continuum, but there was no reason to stop, and so we passed them all by. Besides, swimming downriver with the current makes you feel all is right with the world. The current on the Connecticut was not especially strong that afternoon; as we floated with it downstream, it was almost imperceptible. Had we been trying to swim upriver, its strength would have been more apparent. Still, it gave us subtle affirmation of our direction, and it was impossible at that moment not to indulge in a sense of contentment with the physical world, as though some larger order of things was well within reach. Six weeks earlier I had celebrated my fiftieth birthday. My friends had treated me to a session with an astrologer, who had situated my life and its present circumstances into the grand alignments and movements of the planets and their arc across the sky, but it was drifting midstream down the Connecticut River that day that most confirmed—if such a thing is possible—a sense of affinity with the grander scheme of things.

In his essay "Walking," Thoreau wrote, "I believe that there is a subtile magnetism in nature, which, if we unconsciously yield to it, will direct us aright." This, of course, is Thoreau at his most maddening and preposterous. Anyone who has ever seen a forest demolished by a bolt of lightning, seen the earth swallow their home in an earthquake, or been filled with terror as they are swept from shore in a riptide knows that yielding to the "subtle magnetism" in nature can also lead to an unceremonious and quick end. Still, it seems to be in our nature to believe that if we follow the natural course of things, we will be acting in some conformity to a grander and better scheme than any single imagination can devise. And while walking no doubt can be an exercise that abets this belief, when you are swimming down a river you are as inclined as is humanly possible to put your faith in the subtle magnetism of nature; to believe that you are directed as aright as can ever be.

I once saw an artist's rendering, a photograph that had been created electronically, that converted New York City's High Line into a 7,920-foot-long swimming pool. The Viennese artist Nathalie Rinne had transformed the remnants of the abandoned elevated railway that currently threads its way through Manhattan's West Side into the ultimate urban fantasy, a turquoise lap pool a mile and a half long. The power and resonance of her image did not have simply to do with the captivating incongruity of transforming a railroad bed into an urban river, or of reconstructing solid lengths of steel into rippling water, or even the sheer magnitude of such a project as constructing this artificial river. Rather, I think it had most to do with setting out this straight line of water, offering the possibility of some sublime sense of alignment, and confirming that same sense of subtle magnetism that Thoreau spoke of so hopefully.

Besides, drifting downstream with the current can't help but induce a kind of meditative state. And it occurred to me that a river is a good place to do some reading. In ancient China, serpentine streams were sometimes constructed for the play of literary games. Scholars and poets would gather, positioning themselves at appointed bends in the stream. The host would then name the subject of a poem, then float a cup of wine down the stream to the first guest, who would compose the first line of the poem, sip the wine, then send both down the stream to the next guest. As the cup floated from bend to bend and guest to guest, so too was the poem completed.

Such choreographed rituals seem far from anything we might practice today, yet there is an appealing logic to the way the poem is composed as it travels downstream. Words and water are natural colleagues; it is why so many people love to read in the bathtub. Recently, I heard of a publisher who, recognizing the collegiality of words and water, perfected the art of waterproof bookbinding with a technology he calls Durabook. The submersible, and apparently eco-friendly, books are made not with any sort of laminated paper, but with sheets of polypropylene, and use glues and threads that can withstand prolonged exposure to water. Predictably enough, the first books from this press leaned toward the erotic, with titles like *Wet* and *Aqua Erotica*. Waterproof children's books are already on the market, but to my mind, it's an idea that invites further literary, if not technological, development. Surely biography, the narrative of human life, is a genre that lends itself to the attention of a reader drifting downstream.

But tranquillity and trepidation are made for each other, and as quiet as the river seemed, there was something about such full immersion that brought its own sense of apprehension. From the dyke, the riverscape below us had appeared distant and serene. Even the powerboats cruising down it seemed part of a placid waterscape. But once we were immersed in it, those same powerboats, the changing course of the channel, the opaque blackness of the river where its bed suddenly dropped away, the knowledge that this river was found to have a gaping abyss in its midst—all of these converged to create, if not a sense of outright danger, one of faint uneasiness. Although the factories are long gone from this stretch of river, the dumping of industrial contaminants remains an indelible part of its history. The waste from arms factories, timber operations, paper mills, and tanneries were all flushed into the river for generations, and their legacy, too, contributes to the sense of disquiet. I have heard accounts of the water in the Connecticut River running red in areas below the factories tanning leather, and in her letters, the poet Edna St. Vincent Millay talks about growing up on the banks of a river in Camden, Maine. Upstream from her house was a textile mill, and often, she recalled, the water of the river would run with a rainbow of colors from dyes used by the mill. Reading her words today, one can only imagine the toxicity of that rainbow. But in her image I can see the convergence of beauty and danger that humans have always found irresistible.

In his meditation on beauty, George Santayana wrote that beauty is "an affection of the soul, a consciousness of joy and security, a pang, a dream, a pure pleasure. It suffuses an object without telling why; nor has it any need to ask the question . . . It is an experience; there is nothing more to say about it." Perhaps the components of beauty can never be fixed. On any given day, any one of us may altogether reconsider and redefine the criteria for what it is, exactly, that confers beauty on any given object or place or person. Surely the capacity to give pleasure is essential to beauty. That morning on the Connecticut River, the components of beauty also included an illusory sense of fit with the natural world, the elusiveness of the shifting channel, and a subtle sense of fear. But there was something else too, and that was the knowledge that this was my mother's river. One of the great gifts of the natural landscape is the way in which it connects us to other people, often those lost to us or gone entirely.

Now, when I think back to how we swam down the river that afternoon, and to Steinberg's drawing of a river that realigned the cities on this earth to conform to his own personal geography, I consider how my mother's Connecticut River might exist in her imagination if she were alive today. Every drop, every crease of its current, every shadow on its surface would be true to the river as it runs today; its channel would shift, its willows bend toward the surface, its bed drop away into a sudden abyss. But what is constructed along its banks might also include the veranda of a house in Bangkok, a grove of mango trees, a Manhattan brownstone, a few acres of woodlands in upstate New York, and a beach on Cape Cod.

As a young married woman, my mother had lived in Japan for several years, and while there, she grew to love Japanese stone gardens, or *karesansui*. These are minimal landscapes distinguished most by the fact that they are dry; stones and rocks, unchangeable, are thought to reflect eternal life. And so the placement of a single rock might represent an island or a mountain, white stones might be raked into a rippling pattern to evoke a flowing river, or flat blue stones laid against each other to suggest the current of a flowing stream. My mother found the study of *karesansui* deeply rewarding, and years later, after she had returned to the United States, she often arranged these small stone gardens herself. In upstate New York, we would often find on the dining room table a shallow, rectangular ceramic bowl containing a small composition of bonsai, moss, and fine white sand combed into small rivers. Even toward the end of her life, when a brain tumor had made simple speech difficult and movement nearly pointless, these small stone gardens and rivers held her interest.

Her *karesansui* books are still in my library, and I have read their directives for how one might construct a small, abstract river. "The split stones for the stream bed indicate its quiet nature and great depth," one says. And another: "The white sand describes an expansive river where islets seem to float and points of land seem to push out." And elsewhere: "The boat-shaped stone under the stone bridge on the right expresses the repose of the stream." I read these instructions and try to remember the specifics of the small rivers she constructed for so many years, but I can't recall where the river started or ended or whether there was an abyss.

I know that what we think of as having beauty often has to do with how memory distills human experience, and it is easy to imagine that she found great beauty in a rippling pattern of white stones simply because when these recalled the currents and bends of the Connecticut River, they gave some solace to a young wife continents away from home. And I wonder now if the reason she believed that the Connecticut River was the most beautiful river on earth was that she had found a way to take the river with her.

The Susquehanna River

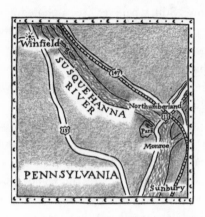

THE DAY I DROVE to Sunbury, Pennsylvania, happened to be the thirty-fifth anniversary of the Apollo Moon Landing. The airwaves were full of reminiscences, and driving across the Pennsylvania farmland, I listened to stories about pool parties and barbecues, about family gatherings where generations crowded onto the living room sofa, and about lawn parties where the family black-and-white TV was set up outdoors with a series of extension cords. One woman remembered a first date that night with the man who later became her husband, recalling how that evening was an excursion into the unknown in every way imaginable.

I remembered my own experience of that night. Operating on some conventional teenage contrarian impulse, my boyfriend and I had decided we could best honor the event by looking at the moon directly rather than through some artificial televised filter, and at the appointed hour we sat in a cornfield gazing at the orb—which, of course, looked as it does on any night. What we had talked about was as preposterous as it was serious; he had labored to explain to me the difference between agnosticism and ignosticism, the belief that questions about a supreme deity are so unknowable, they are best regarded as nonsense. Still, whenever I see a photograph of that grainy televised image of Neil Armstrong stepping onto the moon, I hear some echo of those words, and now, thirty-seven years later, I realize how indelibly that conversation has been imprinted on the event. And I still operate on the belief that the unknowable is worth consideration and conjecture.

But we had gone indoors quickly, then, to join our friends clustered around the television. Listening to the radio now, I was struck by the social aura of that evening so many years ago, and people's impulse to witness that event in gatherings and groups, as though watching a man go farther away than anyone had ever gone before was something best done together. Witnesses to any human endeavor are likely to become accomplices in one way or another. Those people encountered on the periphery of experience often help to define it in some random, but still essential, way. Their expectations and reactions, their fears and exhilaration, and whatever else may occur on the margins all become interwoven into the event, their observations and thoughts often becoming inseparable from the event itself.

Or so it seemed over the next few days as I looked for a place to swim in the Susquehanna River. I got directions from an attendant at the Citgo station, heard the advice of a park ranger, and listened to a warning from a store clerk, and their voices all became a kind of Greek chorus, resonant with warning and admonition, and I knew early on that what Onni and I ended up doing would in one way or another be measured by their words. What it came down to was this: No one wanted to have much to do with our swim; no one on the

edge of the river seemed to think there was anything to be gained
from getting in it.

The shifting riverbed and abyss of the Connecticut River had dal-
lied with our sense of fear, offering up their unseen hazards as a part
of the river's beauty and allure. But the Susquehanna addressed our
fears more directly. The abuses of the Connecticut River are generations old: farming pesticides, runoff from mills, human waste. But the
Susquehanna was more single-minded. The river begins near Coopers-
town, New York, and flows some 440 miles, with its central branch
from upstate New York meeting the shorter western branch from
western Pennsylvania at Sunbury in central Pennsylvania. It is joined
by numerous other tributaries as it flows across the state and then
through Maryland, before it finally empties into the Chesapeake Bay,
North America's largest estuary. And from what we heard, the course
it runs may as well also serve as a timeline of toxicity.

The western branch that flows from the mountains of Pennsylvania has been awash for generations with residual acid from abandoned mines. The northern branch from New York has been dirtied
by generations of waste from industrial cities such as Binghamton,
Scranton, and Wilkes-Barre. Both branches suffered agricultural pollutants, and both have been fouled by sewage that seeps out of aging
municipal treatment plants. The confluence of the two branches in
Sunbury, then, might have been a confluence of pollutants as well.
And downstream in Harrisburg is the Three Mile Island nuclear
power plant that in March 1979 came within a half hour of large-
scale meltdown, allowing the river to claim its place in history as the
site of America's first nuclear crisis. A combination of poor design,
faulty equipment, and human error had led to a partial core meltdown in the reactor, and the subsequent release of radioactive gases
necessitated the evacuation of some hundred thousand residents.

Landscape acquires its identity through generations of experience,
so while the river has been in recovery in the twenty-seven years that
have passed since the Three Mile Island crisis, for many it still generates

the perception of full-service, multigenerational, multiple-source pollution; its legacy as a tainted waterway hostile to humans persists. Which is probably why we shouldn't have been surprised to be warned off the river as repeatedly as we were. By the time we found a way into the river, Onni and I felt almost as endangered as the river itself.

It had been our hope to swim near Sunbury, where the conjunction of the two branches of the river form a wide lake, and I had a day to scout out a good place to swim before I met Onni that night. There is something innately appealing about the place where any two rivers meet, a landscape of peaceable merging. Long before Pennsylvania was ever settled by Europeans, this spot had been recognized by Native Americans and had served as a strategic location for the Iroquois and Delaware nations. Twelve different Indian trails were said to radiate from this spot, leading to all points of the compass, and some of the roads used today conform to those ancient paths. So while the confluence of rivers today may represent an intersection of pollutants, it also can't help but evoke some kind of antique harmonic convergence. Who wouldn't want to swim here?

A mile or so below Sunbury is the Adam T. Bower Dam, a construction that is put in place each summer to raise the water level several feet, creating Lake Augusta, a three-thousand-acre lake for fishing, boating, and waterskiing. With a 2,700-foot span, the Fabridam is an inflatable dam: Its seven, connected thick laminated rubber and nylon tubes are filled with air each May and deflated each November. Because it stops water not with stone or concrete but with air, it tries to suggest that our interventions with nature can have a less damaging touch, and the impermanence of this dam makes it seem more river-friendly. While it is possible for annual systematic flooding to adversely affect river life—the root systems of trees near the shoreline can *still* be damaged, fish habitats can *still* be degraded, and river sedimentation can *still* be prevented from washing downstream—the inflatable dam nonetheless remains an example of a new technology that offers a way to leave a lighter imprint.

Swimming in the lake created by the dam seemed at first to be in the realm of possibility. The attendant at the Citgo station in town told me, "I grew up here. There are lots of places up and down the river you can go in. Just drive around. You'll find them." But, in fact, I didn't. Certainly I didn't get much encouragement from the Greater Susquehanna Valley Chamber of Commerce in Shamokin Dam just below Sunbury. "It's not legal. But you can swim wherever you want," I was told. "Some people even jump off the railroad bridge in Sunbury." As that is an active railroad, I wasn't quite certain what the advice was. Not that it mattered. By then, I was used to the way people, especially those holding some official office, contradicted themselves, managing to say all at once, "You can't do it, you shouldn't do it, but people do it, and you probably will too."

I figured the marina at Shikellamy State Park might be a good place to start. Located at the southern tip of Packers Island, which lies at the mouth of the river's north and main branch, the park is at the center of the confluence, and its shaded groves of locust, silver maple, and oak trees speak to the richness of the river sediment. But both the park and marina seemed eerily deserted for a summer afternoon, so I continued on my way, driving the brief perimeter of the island. I slowed down at the Sunbury Social Club, a gracious, sprawling white building that might have been an old hotel poised on the river's edge; boats were docked there, and benches were scattered across the lawn. Still, it was late afternoon, and for all the seeming congeniality of its name, the atmosphere of the revelry there seemed undercut by the menace of too much beer. I drove north, up the western branch to Lewisburg, where Bucknell University is located, wondering if I'd have any more luck in a college town, but the waitress at the Bull Run Inn shrugged when I asked her if she knew a good point of river access. "I've never been in the river," she said. The bartender recalled being in the river as a kid, swinging across it and into it on a rope swing, but "It's been years now."

People who love rivers also love to talk about them, but here I found that people who fear rivers love to talk about them too. Or maybe it is the fear they were talking about. I wandered into the Orvis outlet, certain that I would find someone there able to guide us to the perfect swimming spot, but the salesman was quick to tell me, "I wouldn't go near the river as a swimmer. I've been in Sunbury in my kayak, and the bass fishermen in their boats tried to run us down. We almost got killed. I won't go down there anymore." As well as a dire warning, his rush of words resonated with the politics of the river and the long-standing polemics between the kayakers and the bass fishermen who tend to favor powerboats. He looked at me meaningfully, the way experienced outdoors people sometimes do.

I met Onni later that night at the R. B. Winter State Park, and over a late dinner of ramen noodles and red wine, I cataloged the various expressions of blunt discouragement I'd heard. She made it clear to me then that we were not to be defeated. I am not a camper and defer to her in matters of setting up the tent, making a fire, cooking the noodles. I can handle pouring the wine. But her persona as the campground commander now extended to director of overall operations. She was weaving our trip to the Susqhehanna into other trips in the northeast with Sam, who was now of the age to be looking at colleges. So maybe it had to do with helping her son map out his next move, but she was sure that we too had a sense of momentum and purpose.

I know her as someone who allows life to take its course. So much so, that she even changed her name when that was needed. She had been given the name Amy by her parents, but when she joined the union as a young actress, the name Amy Cohen had already been registered. Using her married surname didn't help as that had been registered as well, so she next considered taking the name of her Polish grandmother, Anni. On being told that too had been taken, she threw up her hands and said, "Oh, then just spell it with an *O*," and Onni is now the name she also goes by to most of her friends. Re-

naming herself was at once an improvisational and practical measure. Yet as plastic as she may be even about matters of personal identity, she is as capable of unexpected resolve; if it is the discourse
between the fixed and the fluid that informs the way she lives, she has
made a decision now and it's set.

Which is why she wasn't remotely discouraged when the ranger we
met with the following morning at the park office advised us even
more emphatically against swimming in the Susquehanna. "Rivers are
naturally dangerous," she told us. "Currents and rainfall make it difficult to monitor the river for pollution, so we don't check it the way we
do lakes. I'd stay with the lakes if I were you. I've never been in the river
offshore. I've gone in off boats, and I've fallen in, but never been in offshore." And then she added, "People die in the river all the time."

The heat of the July day was already bearing down on us in the
parking lot, and with it came an oppressive sense of inertia. Our directives thus far had been almost unanimously hostile to the idea of a
river swim. Almost on cue, then, we were given different advice. An
elderly couple standing behind us in line at the ranger's office followed us out in the parking lot. Dan Wheeler and his wife were in a
white truck with a camper on back and were securing their site for
the night. He wore white shorts and a polyester striped shirt, she a
pressed denim outfit and stockings with her sandals. They didn't
have the look of experienced outdoors people, and certainly their
clothes were more Wal-Mart than Orvis. But they had a sense of ease,
pleasure with the outdoors. Dan had heard what the ranger told us
and followed us out into the parking lot as though her dire warning
had somehow offended his sensibilities. "I've been on the river for
most of my life, and I'm still here," he told us. "You'll be fine." He
suggested that we go to a campground in Winfield, a few miles
below Lewisberg. "There's a campground there, with a boat launch.
You should be able to get in there."

His advice was reinforced at the local deli in Lewisberg, where we
picked up some coffee. By then, asking where we might swim had

turned into its own minor subsport, and the fry chef behind the counter displayed more of the now familiar dismissive attitude. "Don't have a clue," he said when we asked where to go for a swim. But the teenage boy behind us in line said, "Try Winfield." And so we did.

The kid picking up his egg sandwich reminded me of all the informal, uncollected, unarchived lore of place. All manners of other river data can be found on the Internet: where to fish for bass, where to rent a canoe or launch a powerboat, the availability of camping sites, hiking routes, and bird-watching trails. But where to swim across the river is a different kind of information that can only be gleaned from more improvisational sources. In a time called the information age, the acquisition of knowledge seems but a matter of finding the right search engine and Google literacy. What we were looking for that July morning came instead from an old camper and was reinforced by a teenage boy buying breakfast before he went to work. Essential information still can come from unlikely sources at unpredictable times.

Driving south on Route 15 we found Winfield, and the River Edge RV camp and marina proved to be its own small suburban settlement. The camp office being shut, we drove on down closer to the river past cluster after cluster of RVs. They had names like *Nomad, Prowler, Sportsman, Wilderness, Legend,* and *Challenger*, but comfortably nestled in their pods, they, in fact, composed a portrait of American leisure. Many were decorated, some with red, white, and blue bunting, others going for a more international look with faux Chinese lanterns. Many of them were fronted by small mowed lawns, others had hanging plants, lawn furniture, clotheslines, all signs of careful housekeeping that suggested these were not nomadic vehicles but fixed residences. Despite the lexicon of high adventure, what this riverside resort conveyed most was a sense of safe domesticity and community.

The proprietor came by on her golf cart and affirmed that. "Some of these people live only ten minutes away," she told me. "These are seasonal rentals. But they come back every year. It's peaceful." She and her husband had retired here themselves to look after the campground. "It was his dream," she tells me, "and I said okay. So here we are. Last year after the hurricane came through, the water came halfway up that building"—she pointed to the restrooms a few feet away—"and a friend of mine said, 'I'll bet you could just cry,' but what can you do? You just watch the river. You just watch it go up, and you watch it go down. What more can you do?"

I was reminded of time spent in Mexico, just out of college, when some friends and I had ended up in a small village on the Pacific coast not far north of Guatamala. La Barra, which translates to "the sandbar," is situated on the edge of a river, the Rio de Colotepec, that drains into the Pacific Ocean. It was February, and the fishermen were preparing to move things out of the four or five small cantinas that lined the river farther up its banks. The buildings, called *choza,* were nothing more than brush shacks with roofs of palm fronds to shelter a few tables, jukebox, and cooler for drinks. But each spring the river rose some twenty feet from the melting snow of the Oaxaca Mountains, and the *pescaderos* would just pull out the extension cords, move the tables, the jukebox, the coolor thirty feet inland, and the river would rise, washing the shacks into the ocean. And why, we were compelled to ask, do you build something that is going to be destroyed year after year, and the reply, though polite, clearly reflected that we were out of our minds for asking it at all. "Look around," we were told, and they gestured to the wide, shallow river framed by mango trees, avocado, palm, and papaya. Where it emptied into the ocean, the river was shallow and wide—several hundred feet wide—a lush sanctuary for birds and wildlife. "There is no place on earth more beautiful than the edge of this river to drink," we were told.

Alcohol or no, there was a logic at play here, a strong argument for the purpose of seasonal architecture and for the restorative value of sitting by the river for a few weeks each year. The brush shacks of La Barra may have been thousands of miles from the RVs at Winfield, but they still shared a geography, that spot to sit by the river when the weather is good. The seventeenth-century French philosopher Blaise Pascal said, "I have discovered that all human evil comes from this, man's being unable to sit still in a room," and that may be true, but I would answer that if that room had a window, and that window a view of the river, human evil would be greatly lessened.

Even back in Sunbury, the pleasures of watching the river are being reevaluated. Deforestation, soil that is not very pervious to water, ice dams, and frequent storms have all made the Susquehanna susceptible to regular flooding, and for decades, the city has been effectively separated from the river by a flood wall. While there are places one can climb the dyke at the wall to see the river, there is little sense of any visual, aesthetic, or environmental integration between river and town. But because of the three-month rise of the river each summer when the dam is inflated, the riverbank has eroded significantly and now needs to be stabilized. The Sunbury Riverfront Plan is being developed to consider a more congenial interface between river and town—possibly including landscaping, plazas, a river walk, an amphitheater. Of the latter, Catherine Scheib, the community development coordinator, said, "But just a slab of concrete is not the renaissance we're looking for," an attitude that reflects a larger national awareness in river communities: Now that the rivers are cleaner and more hospitable than they were a generation ago, the cities and towns along them have become more attentive to the kind of planning that allows for active river use.

No one disputes the economic incentives in cleaning up the river and reconnecting communities to their rivers. According to the watch-

dog organization American Rivers, "drinking water, waste assimila-
tion, recreational use, electricity production, seafood harvest, tourism
and other benefits of clean water in the Chesapeake Bay watershed
community contribute over $1 trillion to the region's economy" an-
nually. But there are also subtle human gains that are more difficult
to quantify. Living on the edge of a river situates people on a landscape of constant change and flow that seems to do them good. Proximity to the river offers a lesson about the elasticity of time, a
reminder that although we all tend to use time as a way to measure
our lives and the things we do, it is, in fact, imprecise, volatile, unpredictable, a miscreant of its own, passing far too slowly in tiny drops
that can barely be measured, and then, almost without warning,
streaming by in years.

I think about the Hudson River and how it is governed by both
tide and current and how it flows in two directions and how it sometimes even flows in two directions at once, and how this, too, can
enunciate the disparities between psychological time and physical
time. Who among us hasn't experienced the feeling that the past is
gaining on us, while the future is slipping by too quickly, or that
when we are in pain time passes unhurriedly while pleasure mandates that it be fleeting? There is nothing measured or temperate
about time. It has little or no stamina; it is impulsive. It does not pass
at regular intervals, but is as mercurial and unpredictable as you or
me. We may as well take the absurd view of time adopted by Saint
Augustine in the fourth century because the intervening seventeen
hundred years mean nothing: The past is gone, the future nonexis-
tent, and the present of no value because it has no duration. Time
loses count of us just as much as we lose count of it. And yet. Almost
inexplicably, to watch a river flow by affords one a certain peace, or at
least, reassurance, because it elucidates all of this.

I think of my friend Polly who lives in an old converted firehouse on the banks of the Hudson River. If you were on the tele-

phone with her in January, you might hear her say, "Oh, I just saw an eagle land on an ice floe in the river." Or were the conversation to occur in March, she might mention that "this is the first day there has been no ice on the river." Once her husband, Myron, told me out of the blue, "I am watching the *Kent Loyalist*, a 441-foot ocean-going vessel that is bringing in tons of Brazilian plywood to a docking facility in Poughkeepsie. These ships used to come here, but they stopped. Now something is coming back to this town." "It's different from living near a lake or a pond," Polly told me. "There is always a sense of movement. Maybe it's because it's a tidal river, but the movement of the river is constant, both horizontal and vertical. And there is something about having this river in the foreground, and then the train in the background. It helps me in my day, because when I look out there, I see things moving." What happens on the river is part of their life and part of their conversation, something they share with Pennsylvania retirees and fishermen in Mexico.

But swimming in the river is something else. The campground at Winfield offered a wide assortment of games and recreation: horseshoes, badminton, volleyball, and Ping-Pong, hayrides, a gameroom with pinball machines, and bingo. It also sponsored theme weekends and all manners of gatherings, and shortly after our visit, it hosted a Water Weekend that featured water-balloon games, a watermelon-seed-spitting contest, and water-gun war games. Nowhere was swimming in the river included as a part of the activities. Nonetheless, beyond the RV sites, steps led to the riverbank below, and each site had its own way of getting there: a simple set of solidly constructed wooden steps; an iron staircase that looked as though it might have been salvaged from someone's fire escape; and farther down, a set of wide steps supported by some old railroad ties. The Susquehanna River rises substantially each spring, and repairs get made improvisationally. It's all ad hoc. Everyone has their own way of getting to the river.

On the riverbank itself, a series of small wooden piers jutted out into the river. Along with benches and swings, this point of access had a quaint, nostalgic feel to it, as though they had been built at a time when the river was more hospitable. Leisure is a natural attendant to a summer morning, and although our sense of purpose had not necessarily diminished, it only seemed right to idle on one of the little wooden piers before finally diving into the water.

We had been warned off the river so often that by the time we were finally immersed in it, we could almost taste the danger. We had acquired fear in increments: from the waitress, from the park ranger, from the clerk at Orvis. Now, a bubble on the surface of the water could only be the product of contaminants; the natural viscosity of the water became the residual of industrial pollutants; and the buzz of a powerboat far up the river resonated with malice. The water temperature was that of July river water, comfortable and temperate, but it registered on my skin as unnaturally warm. Whatever else may have actually been in the water that morning, the most synthetic component was surely the impression that it was unsafe to swim in, a perception man-made, manufactured, and surely a contaminant of its own. Experience can so easily be shaped by expectation, by what we are told rather than by what we directly encounter, feel, see, taste, hear, and despite all our best efforts that morning, it was hard to shake the conviction that we were swimming through a sea of toxins.

Onni has said on occasion that swimming across rivers gives her a sense of accomplishment; it demands a certain decisiveness. That may be true, but at the same time, the implicit message of any river is that you could swim forever. I realize, then, that sometimes you do things for reasons that contradict each other. When I was growing up, my father used to tell me that it was a good idea to have two reasons for doing any one thing, and it's a game I sometimes play with myself, calculating the number of reasons there are for doing any single thing. But I wonder now how that tally works when the two reasons seem to be contradictory. Does one cancel the other out? Midstream, it occurred to me that such disparities add up to something bigger, the way, for example, you love your children and do whatever you possibly can to draw them close to you and make them feel safe, so that in the end they will be sufficiently independent so as to leave you. Ambiguity is vastly underrated in the catalog of human impulse and behavior, and besides, there are times when such ambiguity is not about uncertainty or hesitation or indecision, but about the conviction that anything can happen.

The current was imperceptible, yet steady and constant. The Susquehanna has been called "a mile wide and a foot deep," but it was narrower than that here and deeper too. We swam to a small island in the middle of the river, a thicket of twisted locust trees with sinuous branches reaching into the river, and then around it, snaking our way through the boughs and to the bank on the other side. And then we just treaded water midriver, the sense of danger languidly dissipating and floating downstream. It was more than benign, this water; it was quietly gracious, just cool enough to make a difference on a July day, just deep enough here and with a current that told you the river was alive, but without threat. Just below us I could see an old metal pipe jutting out of the riverbank. Maybe on a wet day, it would be running with wastewater into the river, but it didn't worry me today. Afterward, we used the shower in one of the campground's bathhouses to rinse off. *Rinse off what?* I couldn't help but wonder, thinking it was possible that we were bathing in recycled river water that was no different from what we had just been immersed in, except it was pouring out of a pipe in the wall.

Somewhere, I suspect, there are hard facts about the safety and swimmability of the river, and I put this later to Dan Alters, water programs manager at the Department of Environmental Protection in Williamsport. He told me that testing on the Susquehanna has, in fact, fallen off in recent years. "We used to monitor the water at hundreds of locations, running a wide variety of tests including bacteria, all sorts of industrial waste, sewage, mine drainage. The new mines are operated pretty well, but there is still runoff from the old deep mines and from improperly or incompletely reclaimed strip mines, so we test for iron, manganese, and aluminum, as the most important metals from coal mines. And we test for acidity and alkalinity, and for how much mud, or sediment, is in the water. We used to have 135 stations at which we tested water quality within the region, which comprises about fourteen counties in north-central Pennsylvania. Now we're down to about a third of that. And it's true that we don't do nearly enough sampling for safe swimming."

The Pennsylvania Department of Health established sampling standards for public swimming areas that specify the number of samples to be taken each week, locations for samples at the swimming area, depth of water, and time frame for testing. It specifies as well that "bathing shall not be permitted in areas where water currents, as determined during the sanitary survey, normally exceed a velocity of three feet per second. Water currents shall be determined and monitored using a hand flow meter or other method acceptable to the Department. The current in each bathing area (shallow, deep, diving) should be measured at approximately the water depth." Small wonder, then, that the official response is that the river is not safe to swim in. "But," Alters added, "I know the risks and know the places and times when swimming in the river poses less of a risk. I do it."

Alters explained that the only thing that's going to hurt you in the river is the sewage—not runoff from mines, not industrial waste, not agricultural pollutants. "The overall health of Pennsylvania waters is excellent, with the notable exceptions located in those areas with acidic mine drainage impacts or intensive farming activities." About ten years ago, his department began to inventory all streams, and that review is now nearly complete. Streams were broken into segments, and the aquatic life of each segment was compared to the standard of what *should* be living in the stream. Water quality was then characterized as impaired, slightly impaired, or not impaired. The assessment concluded that "mining activities, although accounting for many miles of impaired waters, are not a factor in determining the swimming quality of a water, and industrial waste discharges are simply not an issue, and have not been for many years."

Alters's department is currently working with the EPA on wet-weather initiatives that examine municipal sewage systems and their impact on water quality; heavy rains can cause these systems to overflow into the river. He emphasized the basic truth "that people don't want sewage running in their rivers or through their yards." He's found that most communities are willing to invest in better sewage collection and treatment. And although public swimming in polluted rivers has happened for generations, the real danger is not from swimming in the water but from drinking it. Which swimmers, generally speaking, don't. Alters concluded that "people who know what the issues are can swim in the river. You can swim when it's low and clean. Or when it has been dry for three or four days. You can swim in the river if you do it intelligently. There are limitations to everything we do in life."

He qualified that statement later, adding that waterborne diseases from swimming in the river are not to be taken lightly. "When the river is clear and warm, people are going to swim there. And while the risks are far less now than fifty or even ten years ago, we still have a long ways to go before we can declare that the river is swimmable." Alters's measured voice suggests that river safety is as much about common sense as it is about meeting rigorous official standards. The fears are reasonable, he seemed to be saying, but no less reasonable is the expectation of a cleaner river.

Eight months after our swim, I had occasion to revisit the Susquehanna River. I had wanted to see the river before it had been transformed into a lake by the dam downstream, but when I went

in March, two months before the dam was to be inflated, the water
level was unusually high from the recent spring rains; the shape and
dimensions of the water did not seem so different from the summer before, but what was then a lake was now a floodplain. The at-
titudes I encountered on this trip were different from those I had
met with the previous summer. I stopped at the Southside Bait and
Tackle Shop on the east bank of the river to ask when the Fabridam would be inflated. Ken Maurer runs the place, and when I
happened to mention how often we had been warned off the river
months earlier, he gazed over at the river with the expression people
sometimes have when a beloved friend or relative has been tact-
lessly maligned; he seemed at once regretful, protective, then anxious to set the record straight. He sighed and told me, "The guys
who know the river know it's fine. Trout live in this river, brook
trout, brown trout, rainbows. That tells you something about how
clean the river is."

The following morning, I hiked up to an overlook at Shikellamy
State Park, a spot that offers a panoramic view of the place where the
two branches meet. At eight o'clock that morning, the confluence
was without drama; it was barely even perceptible—a skein of ripples, a curling eddy of water, then a stretch of water smooth as steel,
and the two wide currents simply and peaceably merged. The river, I
knew, was brimming with information, but at this particular moment it appeared silent and inscrutable. From that height, it was hard
to read the language of the water or to know whether those surface
disturbances came from the gentle spring breeze or from the contours and topography of the riverbed below.

Yet when I went back later that day and the two rivers were lit by
a noonday sun, it was a different view entirely. Both rivers were still
running high from the recent rains, and the river flowing from the
west was a dense, earthen green, as though it was carrying all the
shades of color derived from the rain and the mountains behind it.

Because the branch coming from the north was a stronger, more forceful river, it carried more mud with it, and its churning waters were thick, miry, and a milky coffee color; where the two rivers flowed into each other there was a clear demarcation line, and the wash of two separate pigments continued to flow separately downstream where they merged beyond my line of vision. "On any given day the rivers take on whatever is happening in their watersheds," Alters had explained to me. "Precipitation occurs irregularly, and the intensity of water runoff is what makes one river more or less clear and the other muddy to one degree or another." From this point of view at this time of day at this time of year, the separate paths of the two currents were visible, their previous uniformity vanished, and all of it a trick of the light.

After my family left Southeast Asia, we eventually moved to the Hudson Valley in New York. The old farmhouse my parents bought and renovated came with a meadow, woods, three apple trees, and a meandering stream. Like kids everywhere would be, I was most drawn to the water. The stream provided endless ways to play: You could wade, build forts and little boats, divert the water into small pools or dam it up completely. Once, I found a small toy horse, made of lead and painted black with a red saddle, that had washed up on its small bank. But what gave the stream its greatest draw was that it was different every day. The contours of its gravel bed were ever shifting. Its water might be high or low, a rock might have toppled into it, or after a heavy storm, a tree across it. In October, it might be clogged with leaves, and in winter whatever happened took place under its thin scrim of surface ice. Squirrels, foxes, raccoons, and other animals came and went. Water changes whatever is around it, and at the same time, it reflects everything that happens around it. Forty years later, I was having lunch with a friend at a fashionable New York restaurant, talking to her about the changing character of American rivers, and when she quoted the Greek philosopher Heraclitus—"You could not step twice into the same river; for other waters are ever flowing on to you"—I found myself thinking not so much about all the rivers that so preoccupied my life during that time, but of that thin stream of water and how it was a different place every day.

That the view of the Susquehanna had changed so dramatically in the course of only a few hours was oddly comforting. Ordinarily we think of finding reassurance in what is constant, but mutability offers its own reassurances, and I think again of the ease with which Onni revised her name and think maybe she knows something about identity being fluid. And I was reminded again not only of the shifting character of the river but of the transient nature of our perceptions, of the way that rivers assume whatever is happening in their watersheds. And I looked at the gigantic two-tone river below me, surging with its varying currents and contrasting sediments, and it made sense to me then that the range of advice we had been given about where to swim ranged from "There is no place to swim" to "You can swim anywhere you want."

Not long after my visit, the organization American Rivers announced that the Susquehanna topped the list of America's Most Endangered Rivers for 2005. The report's summary reads that "throughout the Susquehanna River watershed, aging sewer systems discharge enormous volumes of raw or poorly treated sewage, which eventually flow into the Chesapeake Bay. Unless local, state, and federal lawmakers invest in prevention and cleanup, the Susquehanna will remain among the nation's dirtiest rivers, and more and more of the Chesapeake Bay will become a dead zone." Sara Nicholas, a spokesperson for the organization, elaborated that the Susquehanna tops the list not because it is America's dirtiest river but because it offers such opportunity for reclamation. The problems—not only sewage from outdated and overwhelmed combined sewer outfall systems but also acid mine drainage, nonpoint-source pollutants that stream into the river from no single source, but from a vast and more generalized use of noxious materials such as excess nitrogen and phosphorus from agricultural runoff, and proposed construction of a new dam across the main stem river at Wilkes-Barre—are significant, but the river still sustains an impressive fishery and an abundance of other aquatic resources, so it is hardly "dead."

Nicholas outlined opportunities to benefit the river: a new state bill that would create a one-billion-dollar bond to help finance upgrades for combined sewer outfall systems; a plea to Congress not to cut the State Revolving Loan Fund that finances water cleanups, and an appeal to state and federal regulators in Pennsylvania to rule against the construction of the dam. Asked whether the designation "America's Most Endangered River" may be confusing and contribute further to negative perceptions about the Susquehanna, Nicholas replied that it serves as both "a warning and a message of hope." She hopes that the public will come to recognize both what the problems are and how they can be corrected. I hope she's right.

The formal definition of river safety has to do with monitoring pathogens and measuring the velocity of the current. But our own ideas of safety and danger may be harder to quantify and define, and how we actually come to feel safe in this world is another matter. The object of our fears is rarely what it should be; so often, the things that fill us with dread are barely worth the trouble, while we rush headlong, brazen and oblivious, into things that should instill in us the fear of god. When I was younger, speaking to a roomful of strangers filled me with panic, and my heart would pound, my hands tremble. A garter snake on the front step could reduce me to jelly. But I never blinked when I took up with a fisherman who had just sunk his boat in Alaska's Sitka Sound and had resorted to drinking vodka for breakfast.

The Susquehanna has a legacy of environmental abuse, and certainly there are places where its current is swift and unpredictable. But the river is not unsafe to swim in. I wonder if our sense of safety owes less to the character of the object—or person or animal or place or river—that we fear and more to our fierce determination to choose our fears. It is a paradox of human behavior that we often confront one fear simply by fearing something else.

This, at least, is something I came to suspect when I taught my sons to drive. They had just turned sixteen, and like many parents do at such a milestone, I revisited some of their earlier milestones. "Noel ate his first peach today," I read from the diary we kept during the boys' first year. "Luc took a step." But the week of their birthday was attended by less benign events. We had planned to go to a local shopping mall, where a skate store was selling some boards they wanted, but a weekend idleness had set in, and in the end, we decided not to go. That was a good thing, because later that afternoon, a twenty-five-year-old man went to Best Buy with an AK-47 and fired more than fifty rounds into the store. Two people were hit, though not fatally, and the mall was in lockdown for several hours. Two days after that, a friend of theirs totaled his car. And the following morning, when my sons arrived at school, they saw a crowd of police cars. A student who had been suspended the previous week had made a violent threat toward the school online the night before. All these events occurred in just four days.

After celebrating their birthday, the boys were about the age I was when I was being tutored on the differences between the agnostic and the ignostic, and I wondered what was going through their heads now. Could they understand and accept the rote violence around them, or was it so incomprehensible as to make it pointless to consider? A less abstract exercise was applying for their driving permits, and so we went to the Department of Motor Vehicles. And though it didn't seem that way at first, I realized later that driving lessons were a way for all of us to steady our nerves. The road we were driving along runs down our little valley, Clove Mountain to the west and a lower ridgeline to the east. There was little traffic, and only a few farms and houses. But the woodlands and cornfields are home to deer, rabbit, pheasant, coyote, even an occasional bear. Driving down this valley has always calmed me, and it seemed a good place to learn the rules of the road.

And it was. A pheasant ran out into the road. Luc saw a herd of grazing deer, and I saw his hands tighten, his shoulders stiffen. He had driven with me enough times to know how quickly they could move. It was mid-February, and although there was no snow that week, there was the odd patch of ice here and there. A truck from the local highway department followed us a little too closely. These were the dangers they faced that afternoon, and they were real and genuine dangers; by driving slowly and deliberately, they were learning how to manage them. A deranged man with a semiautomatic weapon in a mall and a high school in lockdown were something else. But if they could learn to avoid the pheasant and dodge the deer, that was a start.

I don't know what else we could have done that week. The ideas teenage boys have about danger are profoundly different from mine. They have little interest in swimming these rivers with me; the quiet current of the Susquehanna would hold little appeal to them. They are skateboarders and snowboarders, and for them danger involves steep concrete stair sets and icy mountain ledges. Were they to have any interest in a river excursion, it would be surfing the *pororoca*. The Tupi Indian word translates as "Great Noise" and refers to the seemingly endless waves, preceded by a deafening roaring sound, that churn through the rivers of the Amazon basin in early spring when tides from the Atlantic Ocean are swept upriver hundreds of miles and collide with the outflow of the river. Surfers congregate on the inland riverbanks to wait for the wave, which can move as fast as twenty miles an hour, with a swell that can be thirty feet high and a duration of up to forty-five minutes. While native Amazonians have surfed the *pororoca* in canoes for generations, tourists now travel there, and surfing tournaments begin with contestants identifying where the unpredictable wave might be found; its whereabouts are often determined by its sound and the sudden activity of birds and other wildlife around it. Once the *pororoca* is located, the surfers must negotiate not only the wave and current but bends in the river, its confining banks, overhanging tree limbs, and the possibility of being swept up a hidden river tributary. And then there are the alligators, anacondas, piranhas, and the occasional leopard. Now there is an epic and fantastic river ride that might meet my sons' standards for danger.

On the road that afternoon with my sons, I was reminded of a road I had seen not long before in a photograph in a magazine. The ad was for a Jeep. With the benefit of some digital darkroom technology, the image of the country road winding through woodlands ablaze in autumn foliage in the foreground of the picture gradually morphed into that of a river meandering through meadows and a pine forest, eventually emptying into a vast lake ringed by snow-capped mountains. "Now you can make the most of every journey," the ad said. The image of the beige Jeep seemed oddly static, and as a visual that might make you want to go out and buy a new car and go on a road trip, it fell short. But the illustration of the blacktop magically transforming itself into a flowing azure river captured something else more successfully. It could have been our country road, I realized, and it could have been the Susquehanna River, and it illustrated precisely how their drive and my swim are part of the same enterprise.

My mother managed to familiarize me with the beauty of the Connecticut River, and I wonder if there is some way I can now pass along this river to my own sons. Or at least what I picked up here. Fear is real. Fear is deep. Fear is profound. But you can also know and learn and choose your fears. I look at Luc's face and think of him a decade ago when he had started school, and I remembered leaving him in the classroom that morning, his small face resolute, his features set in an expression that spelled out his resolve to stay there that morning at that table though he was lonely and afraid. Sometimes when I am at the edge of a river, stepping through the reeds and rocks and into the river's current, I think of his face that morning and know that I am also trying to find these skeins of nerve so that I can braid them together into the kind of courage that will be required for endeavors that go beyond swimming on a bright summer morning. It is impossible not to anticipate greater fears, the ones that may come with age or the news that the lump is not benign or the death of people I love. When that happens, I hope to imagine his face at the table that morning or his steady attention as he was learning to drive.

And I think of the park ranger telling us to stay out of the river, of the waitress who had never been in the river, of the kayaker who wouldn't go near the confluence of rivers in Sunbury, and of the *pororoca* surfers waiting and listening for their wall of water. We all want the chance to calculate our own risks, to decide for ourselves what scares us, to just get the knack of identifying what is worth fearing. And I hear Dan Alters, who has been testing the waters of Pennsylvania for thirty years, advising, "Do it intelligently. There are limitations to everything we do in life." Maybe it's a matter of calculating those limitations; or of understanding that through some process of reduction, you can find a way to *feel* safe in the river or on the road or in the world, which in the end may be the way to make those places safe.

I think of Onni's son, Sam; the week he started his freshman year of high school, the towers of the World Trade Center fell six blocks from his home. For many months afterward Onni and her family found themselves living in a place with air that was unsafe to breathe. I have thought of her as someone who is fearless, but I wonder now if it is only because I cannot fully comprehend her fears. Later, when I asked her about it, she would tell me what she remembered most clearly of that morning was "the stunningly lovely rain of glittering paper scraps and what appeared to be flocks of birds catching the light, which was so crystal clear that day. In one instant I realized that what I was seeing was a body, one single body falling through space, and at that instant the picture froze, much in the way that in the days of film production, the sprockets would get stuck on one frame, leaving that image and going no further in the narrative. My own way of quantifying the unquantifiable then, I suppose, was reducing the infinite to one."

The Hudson River

IN GRAPHIC DESIGN, the word *river* refers to the white space between words that sometimes connects in a rippling vertical pattern
down the printed page. Such a river is to be avoided because it can
interrupt the flow of text in an irregular pattern and distract the
reader's eye from the horizontal progression of the printed words.
But just as it may be a distraction, that space between words also con-
firms their meaning. If a river can both separate and connect on the
printed page, it is capable of doing this all the more in the natural
world. I am beginning to understand that if my intent to swim across
rivers began with wanting to cross a divide, it has now drifted toward
another, different purpose which has to do not with crossing the path
of the river but with following it. "Somehow the line of the river is

that line that I follow," says the artist Andy Goldsworthy, and it seems obvious now that following the path of the river is as important as crossing it. It is the way the unexpected can sometimes take hold of intent, thwarting it, subverting it, transforming it in the same way an argument can sometimes become a pact. A river can connect every bit as effectively as it divides.

Maybe because there is something so essentially primal about swimming, I have always thought of it as a solitary endeavor. In ordinary circumstances that's what it tends to be. Swimming is, by nature, asocial; in the subaquatic realm, the human community is peripheral. The very substance of water puts you at a remove, and even when you are swimming with another person, it confers a solitude. One doesn't speak, one can't hear, and while swimming is innately sensual, some of your senses are nonetheless in temporary suspension. Though you may not be alone, it is easy to believe that you are. Swimming demands social disengagement, and unless one happens to be involved in some kind of synchronized swimming, contact and conversation are impractical. All of which is part of its beauty. In *Haunts of the Black Masseur: The Swimmer as Hero*, the British writer and swimmer Charles Sprawson goes farther, suggesting that "the swimmer's solitary training, the long hours spent semi-submerged, induce a lonely meditative state of mind. Much of the swimmer's training takes place inside his head, immersed as he is in a continuous dream of a world under water. So intense and concentrated are his conditions that he becomes prey to delusions and neuroses beyond the experience of other athletes."

I don't know that I would agree with swimmers being delusional. That swimming is solitary and rhythmic tends to put the swimmer in a reflective frame of mind where the water can comb out the concerns and anxieties of ordinary life, and possibly there are times that shutting out anxieties could be called delusional. But certainly the sense of distance one feels underwater confers a kind of comfort. While I once enjoyed listening to a Mendelssohn concerto with a set of aquatic earphones that I had borrowed from a friend, it was an aberrant moment. It is the silence and remove of being underwater that I value most.

Still, whether it was Sprawson's discouraging diagnosis or simply the innate impulse to test one's own assumptions, I was assailed from time to time with the notion of swimming as a communal, possibly even social, activity. Certainly swimming and eroticism are natural colleagues. I can think of no other sport that is so innately sensual. It is not only in the way the water caresses your skin, but in the way it is all about reaching as far as you can. Swimming is about touching the surface of the water and drawing yourself across it, it is about remove and submersion, and sometimes it is also about submitting to the strength and current and direction of the water. With all of this comes some essential awareness that water is a conduit.

Even Sprawson, once he has established the idea that the swimmer is a lonely neurotic, doesn't hesitate to note that swimming is also an enterprise that can establish a romantic bond and has been cataloged doing exactly that exhaustively by writers through the ages. For Lord Byron, water was just another venue in which to pursue his famous liasons; lame from birth, it was only in the water that Byron felt complete physical freedom, and in swimming that he cultivated emotional attachments to men and women alike. To be Lord Byron's swimming partner was almost certainly to be his lover. The writer Jack London and his wife, Charmian, took long daily swims in the Pacific Ocean that are reflected in the writer's work, and from F. Scott Fitzgerald's Dick Diver to Tennessee Williams's Sebastian, the history of literature is full of swimmers who, for all their delusions and lonely neuroses, find in water the catalyst for erotic attachments. The homoeroticism of men swimming together in the nude has a legacy that dates to ancient Greece, and it continues today in the occasional men's clubs, where, perhaps because it conjures memories of childhood experience, it remains a cherished ritual of male bonding.

If one accepts the idea that swimming can cultivate an erotic bond, surely it can establish other ties as well. It only makes sense that if swimming is an act that can bring with it hope and renewal, it can bring these not only to individuals and to pairs but to entire groups. Roy Webster was an orchardist who moved to Hood River, Oregon, after World War II. Finding that he wanted more exercise than that of simply tending to his pear and apple trees, in 1942 he instituted a Labor Day family swim across the Columbia River. Webster was a member of the Church of the Latter Day Saints, and it was not long before his fellow church members began to accompany him as well. The size of Webster's group grew over the years, and in the mid-sixties he asked the local chamber of commerce to take over the organization of the Roy Webster Columbia River Cross Channel Swim. Today, some 550 swimmers from the age of ten and up, many in wet suits, jump into the sixty-eight-degree water each September for no good reason other than to get some exercise and experience the natural beauty of the Columbia River Gorge.

The swimmers are shuttled to Washington in a paddleboat, and for the duration of their one-mile swim back to Oregon, barge traffic on the river is halted. The swim is supervised by a consortium of the county sheriff's department and coast guard, while flotillas of power-boats, sailboats, kayaks, and canoes escort the swimmers. The swim is not timed; it's not a race, though due recognition may be awarded to swimmers who have traveled the farthest, the oldest swimmer, or the swimmer who has participated for the most consecutive years. The congenial spirit of the swim is reflected in a poem written by Webster, who made his own last cross-river swim when he was eighty-six. (Members of his family continue to do the swim.) Neither a mission statement nor any particularly serious expression of purpose, its plain language reflects Webster's simple goal and reward: *Not a race, nor a contest, but just an achievement / to accomplish a goal—and thus bring appeasement / to the urge that lies dormant in everyone's soul / to do something noteworthy however modest the goal. /*

And so to each swimmer who embarks on the swim— / good luck and good swimming as you respect win.

The annual Hudson River swim that takes place each September in Irvington, New York, is a different kind of community swim. The swim was started in 1991 by Dennis Chillemi, an Irvington police officer who had grown up near the river in Tarrytown, New York. His intent was simply to show people that one could swim in the river and "not come out green and glowing." And when asked how it all started, he said simply, "There was no plan. It just happened by . . . happening." When he was a child, the river had been a place of recreation (probably, he now admits, simply because the kids didn't know any better), and once as a teenager, he had swum across the river with a group of friends on a lark. By 1991, married and the father of seven children, he wanted to swim across it again. Why? "I dunno," he said. "A fitness thing, maybe. The river was just calling." That summer, Chillemi made arrangements for an escort boat and swam from Irvington to Piermont, a distance of three miles across the Haverstraw Bay where the river is exceptionally wide. Once he was done, he realized he could just as easily have swum back again.

Chillemi is one of those people who, having done something once, reflexively imagines how it might be done better the next time. And he keeps at it. When I headed down to talk to him one winter afternoon in February, just as he was beginning to plan the following year's swim, he asked to change the time of our appointment at the last minute. We had decided to meet at a coffeehouse in Tarrytown, but after he got off from work, he had to take one of his daughters to a doctor's appointment, and later on, there was the MS swim meeting. Somewhere in between there was still an hour to meet. It occurred to me as we were talking on the telephone that he was not likely to be the embodiment of the lonely, delusional swimmer. If anything, he might be the embodiment of the old saying that "if you need to get something done, ask a busy person to do it."

After his swim in 1991, Chillemi decided with his wife that the river swim could be repeated, not simply as a fitness exercise or as a feat of individual accomplishment, but to raise money and awareness for a broader cause. The Blythedale Children's Hospital in Valhalla, New York, he knew, needed wheelchairs equipped with respirators for its quadriplegic patients. The following summer, then, not only did he swim across the river, but he swam back again, and the following week he swam the full sixteen miles down the Hudson from the Tappan Zee Bridge to the George Washington Bridge. "I'm going to do it or pass out trying," he had told a local newspaper, and he was photographed passing out as he emerged from the water beneath the George Washington Bridge. "But it changed my life," he said. Maybe more important, it changed some others. A single anonymous pledge for $10,000 had come in after Chillemi spoke on a local radio show, and an additional $15,000 came in from other pledges, enabling the hospital to buy two fully equipped wheelchairs.

Chillemi continued the fund-raising swim for the children's hospital for several more years, but in 1997, when his partner on the police force was diagnosed with multiple sclerosis, both the incentive and stakes changed. When he took his idea for a fund-raising swim to raise money and awareness for MS to the local chapter of the National Multiple Sclerosis Society, the tone of the response was a mixture of skepticism and disbelief. That first year, there were fourteen swimmers who together raised $6,000. By 2004, Chillemi's solitary swim had become a national fund-raising event for the MS Society with some 245 swimmers, 142 kayakers, and 21 support vessels participating to raise over $150,000 to support families and to contribute to finding a cure. We have three goals, Chillemi told me: "To raise money for MS; to promote swimming as a fitness exercise; and to show that the Hudson River is viable again." The three-mile swim from Piermont to Irvington takes about ninety minutes, with kayakers and numerous support boats escorting swimmers as thousands of spectators cheer them on.

It is a highly and necessarily organized event; all swimmers are outfitted with ankle bracelets embedded with an identification chip that keeps track of who's gone in the water and who's come out. Boats anchored midriver chart the swimmers' course, and escort kayaks are assigned to swimmers for individual guidance and direction. Members of the West Point swim team participate both by swimming and crewing kayaks. One cadet challenged his father to join him in the swim, and the latter flew up from Kentucky to do just that. Swimmers with MS participate, as does one blind swimmer and another who is an amputee. "All these stories, all these connections are what keep the swim going," Chillemi told me.

What he tells all of the swimmers in a preswim meeting is this: "You are going to leave with a sense of ownership of this river. You drank that water. You are going to have a real connection to the river. The Hudson River is the largest living entity in New York State. And you're going to feel a real responsibility to take care of it." Chillemi continues to do the swim himself, but he is always the last in the water. "I take my time," he told me. "I get emotional. My wife is on the other side of the river, waiting for me with a cup of coffee. There are a hundred volunteers, but I still worry until everyone gets out of the water."

For Chillemi, the swim is all about solidarity—with community, with a purpose, with the river. His conviction that swimming can be an exercise in sociability—genuine sociability, that is, in which people gather not for congeniality but in the pursuit of a common goal—is contagious. And both Chillemi himself and his account of the MS swim can't help but underscore the fact that a river swim that is driven by some larger sense of purpose exceeds the thrill of individual accomplishment. Though tempted to join that swim, I find that I have a greater allegiance to the swim suggested two years earlier by Pete Seeger. Since that September morning when I had been looking for an escort boat and been introduced to him instead and heard his plan for the Hudson River equality swim, the idea of a collective river swim on that particular stretch of river that I am so familiar with had lodged itself in my mind, and when the swim was to finally take place, it seemed to be the time to consider the rewards of social swimming. Possibly, I imagined, the wide waters of the Hudson might confer a broader understanding of communality.

If you are a swimmer and if you are equipped with a sense of purpose, a river may be what you want; its flow can support single-mindedness and reconfirm conviction and determination. Martin Strel, a music teacher from Slovenia, swam the entire 3,004-kilometer length of the Danube River in 2002 simply in an effort to promote peace, friendship, and clean water. And from July to September 2002, he took on the entire length of the Mississippi River. That was also the tenth anniversary of the diplomatic ties between the United States and the independent Republic of Slovenia, and it was Strel's intention to swim ten hours a day, day after day, until he had swum the entire 2,320-mile course of the river to further the alliance between the two countries as well as again promoting "peace, friendship, and clean waters."

Christopher Swain is a swimmer from Burlington, Vermont, who has made it his mission to swim American rivers to raise environmental awareness. He is not beyond putting his health at risk. He has swum the entire length of the Columbia River (1,243 miles), the Hudson River (315 miles), the length of Lake Champlain (125 miles) and the Charles River (80 miles). Along the way, he has encountered everything from human to nuclear waste, lightning storms, attacks by lamprey eels, collisions with boats, and toxic blue-green algae. Swimming the Charles River, he navigated his way around abandoned cars, refrigerators, washer, dryers, old tires, along with industrial pollutants and sewage; he also met with schoolkids and state legislators and led trash cleanups. His belief that the Hanford Nuclear Reservation in southeastern Washington is "the most contaminated piece of land in the entire western hemisphere" did not stop him from swimming the section of the Columbia that flows through it simply to make the statement that "we should do something here."

In the Hudson River, Swain swam through Class IV rapids, PCBs, and sewage. And again he met with schoolkids, teachers, government officials, and representatives from GE. He also met with Pete Seeger, whose parting words to Swain were documented on his journal posted on his Web site: "Remember that you are part of a worldwide movement, that you are just a grain of sand . . . the world will be saved by millions of small things, and these things will be done by people like you." Swain confessed to feeling unworthy of the compliment, but then he added, "I realize that Pete is giving me something else. Something I can spend the next fifty years living up to."

Swain's experience with Seeger was not unusual; it's hard to spend any time at all with Seeger and not come away with some sense of resolve. And certainly the Newburgh-to-Beacon swim that finally took place in September 2004 was for a cause that was easy to support. It had long been Seeger's vision to build a river pool, an enclosed area within the river—and using river water—for people to safely swim and wade in. From the 1880s to the 1920s, just such pools, resembling square donuts, were common around Manhattan. Wooden, cagelike structures with adjacent changing rooms and walkways, the floating bathhouses were used by urban immigrant communities as bathing and recreational facilities. In Europe, many such pools are still in use, especially in Switzerland and in some Scandinavian countries. But as Seeger, who lives in Beacon, New York, says, "By 1928 or so, the water [of the Hudson] was too polluted, so the pools were discontinued. But since then, a lot of people said, 'One of these days, we'll have those pools again. We've got to clean up the river.'"

Seeger's conviction that the Hudson River should be available to swimmers was instilled in him as a child. "I swam in the Hudson, near Nyack, as a boy in the nineteen twenties," he told me, and there was speculation that the typhoid his brother contracted then came from swimming in the contaminated waters. He brushed aside any interest I had in how his commitment to river stewardship might have had its roots in this childhood experience, laughing quietly at my efforts toward such pointless self-scrutiny. He continued: "The pollution came mostly from sewage then. Industry didn't have too many chemicals. Primary treatment plants were all most towns had, which means all they did was take the lumps out. Secondary treatment plants didn't come about in most places until the early seventies. The water just got dirtier and dirtier." But even then, he remembered, kids were swimming in the river. "Kids swim wherever they can, you know. I remember coming up on the Dayliner with my daughter right after she was born in New York City in 1948 to take her to see her grandparents in Woodstock. When the Dayliner stopped in Poughkeepsie, people would toss coins overboard and watch as the local kids dove in after them, flickering around in the water."

Some thirty years after the passage of the Clean Water Act, the waters of the Hudson are clean enough to swim in again. The river is again a habitat for striped bass, shad, sturgeon, blue crab, and eel. But river reclamation isn't limited to environmental restoration. Commercial concerns have been attentive to the development potential of a cleaner river, and many people worry that such development may lead directly from polluted industrial waterfronts to overpriced condos with river views, without so much as a nod to public use and access. The construction of a river pool, then, would accomplish a variety of objectives: For those people scared of swimming in open water, it would provide a safe way to swim in the river. It would also provide easy public access to the river, educate the public about river stewardship, promote swimming and physical fitness in the natural environment, and construct a prototype pool for other river communities around the country to emulate.

The architect Meta Brunzema was one of the people Seeger had referred to who looked to reestablishing the tradition of a river pool. A 1990 graduate of Columbia University's School of Architecture, she had worked in the offices of Gwathmey Siegel and Steven Holl. Less interested in the high-end residential and office renovations that came her way, and believing that "architecture can change the world,"

Brunzema opened her own office in Hell's Kitchen in 1998 to focus on public projects, particularly community work in the neighborhood and waterfront planning. Brunzema's original design for a river pool took its cues from a feasibility study done by the Parks Council for a floating recreation center, a barge parked next to a city pier with a hole cut out of it to form a pool. Because the shadow of the barge would be detrimental to the river's aquatic life, Brunzema developed a design more like a transparent, plastic bowl suspended in the water. As she explained, however, "My goal was to have this be as progressive as possible. But in their effort to promote clean water, the environmentalists told me they wanted the river pool to use actual river water instead of filtered water."

Her second plan looked more directly to its nineteenth-century predecessors—but rather than the square wooden donut, the sixty-six-foot diameter pool was to be reinforced by steel rings along with stainless steel netting at the sides and a steel net at the bottom. Ramps from the shore would lead to the pool. With its framework only partially submerged in the water, the pool would allow swimmers to be fully immersed in the river water while being kept safe from its currents and tides. The pool would also have a seventy-five-foot extension that provided lanes for swimming laps. To top it off, the lightweight pool had a collapsible design so it could be folded for storage during winter months.

A short film about Brunzema's work was subsequently shown at a waterfront festival in New York City. Seeger was in attendance that day, and as Brunzema recalled, "He flipped. He fell in love with this round pool, maybe because it looks kind of like a banjo." Within days of seeing her plan, he contacted Brunzema to articulate both his own excitement and design refinements, chief among them the inclusion of a toddler pool. Seeger suggested that the riverfront in his own town might provide the ideal site for the first pool. His comments also addressed more formal design considerations: "He liked the fact that it was round," Brunzema says. "He thinks there are already too many square things in the world."

Working with assorted federal, state, and local agencies—the U.S. Army Corps of Engineers, the Department of Environmental Conservation, New York State's Coastal Management Program, and the local Department of Health—to determine the criteria for permeable pool enclosures, Brunzema was faced with extensive water-quality-testing requirements. Because the river is an estuary, construction also required environmental impact studies. Unphased, she determined that a twenty-foot-diameter wading pool should be built as a prototype to test both engineering and environmental concerns, saying, "I believe that there is a design solution to everything." With partially submerged steel fencing sides that are open to the flow of river water and a floor constructed of steel netting, along with flotation seats on its perimeter that offer spectacular river views, the smaller prototype has been designed to test both the structural capabilities and safety concerns of the larger pool. To raise some of the ninety-five thousand dollars needed for the construction of a prototype to be installed in summer 2006, the Beacon Sloop Club, which counts Seeger among its members, had organized the one-mile fund-raising swim from the city of Newburgh across the river to Beacon.

Seeger is fond of saying that "you can't expect people to fight for a cleaner river until they learn to love it," a theory that the town of Beacon is well positioned to test. While quaint villages of eighteenth-century brick townhouses and clapboard cottages are part of the architectural history of the Hudson River, no less authentic are the industrial wastelands that habitually separate these towns from the river. From the middle of the nineteenth century, coal and lumber operations up and down the Hudson, along with tanneries, mills, foundries, and factories, all depended on the river for the transport of supplies and materials. Their goods could be carried to their destinations on steamboats and barges, while their waste materials along with day-to-day garbage were routinely flushed into the river. Then in the late 1840s, the Hudson River Railroad was constructed along the riverbank, and the waterfront functioned as an industrial corridor until the middle of the next century, when the commercial traffic of ships and railroads was largely assumed by trucks on a burgeoning interstate system. But by then, the riverfront was derelict and degraded.

Certainly that was the case in Beacon, which had been cut off from the river for generations. Here, industrial fills in the nineteenth and twentieth centuries had created space for factories, salt and coal storage sites, a junkyard that had left its residue of heavy metals (among them arsenic and lead), and an oil storage terminal that had saturated the ground with petroleum. As Alan Zollner, a member of the sloop club and president of River Pool at Beacon, Inc., told me, "Thirty years ago, living near the river was something no one wanted to do. That was the poor section of town." In more recent years, the transformation of the old Nabisco packaging factory into the Dia:Beacon museum has been one celebrated effort to redress that. Another waterfront project proposes multiuse development with a park, hotel, restaurants, and docks for nonmotorized boats. But it is the proposed river pool just upstream that will actually get people into the water.

Which is how I came to find myself on a windy, gray September day on the Newburgh pier directly across the river from Beacon with Meta. Like Seeger, who believes music can change the world, Meta believes that architecture can be its own kind of activism, and she decided to swim, along with sixty-two others, ranging in age from thirteen to seventy-eight. Some thirty-five kayakers were working as spotters, a coast guard escort was on hand, and river traffic had been stopped for the duration of the swim. Slack tide was around two o'clock that afternoon, so the swim was planned for one thirty. One of the organizers explained to us as we prepared to dive into the river, "We'll start with the slow swimmers. The medium-speed swimmers can go in, then the fastest swimmers. That way, everyone will reach the other side at almost the same time." The set of instructions

echoed Seeger's visionary outline that I had first heard two years earlier, and while such enforcement tactics for making things equal on
this earth almost never work out as planned, something else that
brings out the best in people was at work that day.

There was, for example, the reluctance among swimmers to rate
themselves by ability; it seemed tacitly understood that identifying
yourself as a fast or slow swimmer directly contradicted the egalitar-
ian spirit of the afternoon. While one swimmer in a wet suit and a
pair of high-tech, chartreuse goggles admitted to being a fast swimmer, I noticed he was also anxious to be in the water, and rather than
wait to go in last, he dove in somewhere in the middle of the crowd.
Another swimmer reluctantly admitted to being fast, then added
quietly, "But today, I think I'd rather do it slowly." And those who
felt they might be the slower swimmers seemed disinclined to go to
the head of the line and jump in the water first, as though the knowledge that they were sure to finish last necessitated that they jump in
last as well; swimming being the leisurely activity it is, the pride and
pleasure to take things slowly is not easily relinquished.

Who of us, when confronted unexpectedly and directly, knows
best how to identify our skills and talents? Who was fast and who
was slow? Possibly, this manner of self-evaluation can be taken seriously in a therapist's office or in some corporate human resources department, but for those of us standing on a windy pier in Newburgh,
New York, on the verge of swimming across the Hudson River, any
semblance of the assured self-regard we might possess in other of
life's pursuits had vanished with the wind and the current. That self-
knowledge, an uncertain science to begin with, can come and go so
fleetingly seemed strangely comforting, and it only made sense that
in the face of nature, the sweep of the long, gray river and the cut of
mountains above it, what we seemed to be so certain of in ourselves
was suddenly evanescent. In the end, we just jumped into the river in
random groups of four or five.

The river was choppy that afternoon. Visibility was low. The natural turbidity of the river, a product of its aquatic life, made it difficult to see anything underwater, and when I lifted my head out of the water, the waves and whitecaps obscured the view of the shoreline as well. If this river were a book, it was dense, obscure, difficult to read. Some rivers have a brilliant clarity; they are translucent, quick, clear about themselves and where they are going and where they are taking you. Others, like the Hudson, have a thickness and opacity, as though there is too much type on the page to take it all in. The pages are long and packed with intricate information, and even at the end of the page, you may not be quite sure of what you've read. Its narrative begins as a pond on the side of Mount Marcy in the Adirondacks, and the clear mountain stream running from it ends up as a tidal channel in the Atlantic Ocean. Its character, never fixed, is transformed during its passage from freshwater to saline, from a thin, winding stream to a broad straight channel. It has a tide and a current, and it flows both ways; sometimes it flows both ways at once.

And still, there was a sense of lightness on the day of our swim. Maybe it was the river's proximity to the ocean, the fact that it is tidal and carries the distant taste of seawater, or maybe it was just the thrill of finally being in the water, but a sense of natural buoyancy seemed to carry us across the swells and through the whitecaps and their confetti of spray. And if those made it difficult to gauge distance and direction without stopping and pausing to regain bearings, if those slowed the rhythm of the swim, that wasn't altogether a bad thing. Constantly stopping was also a way of taking measure of how far we had come and how far we had yet to go. Trying to judge distance across water is an improbable exercise. I didn't know whether I had swum a quarter mile or a third or was even coming close to a half. And despite the fact that we were swimming at slack tide, there was a slight tug of current upstream that seemed to further obscure whatever sense of distance and direction I was hanging on to.

Our route across the river had once been that of the Newburgh-Beacon ferry service, said to be one of the longest-running ferries in American history. Launched for the first time in 1743 under a charter from King George II, it served as an essential conduit for military men and their supplies during the American Revolution. Later, it served the river's commerce and after that tourism and leisure, running continuously until 1963, when the Newburgh-Beacon Bridge was opened. Swimming at a place in the river with such a legacy of transit was reassuring; though our predecessors had been on, rather than in, the water, that afternoon they were an unseen community of colleagues.

On the far side of the river at Beacon, the organizers at the sloop club had hung an enormous banner in a rainbow of bright colors, our presumed landmark and finish point, but midriver, it was barely visible amid the buildings and boats lining the Beacon marina. Landmarks behind us in Newburgh—some old shipping containers, the old brick factory buildings converted into restaurants, a church steeple—were no more distinct. They had quickly become irrelevant, and it was the steel sections making up the wide span of the Newburgh-Beacon Bridge just to the north that became my measure and point of reference. Possibly, that was in accordance with some universal law: The point of departure that seems so grounding and significant when you are leaving a place becomes vague and indistinct once you're gone.

I paid attention to the rhythm of my breathing now, and that became my second measure, evanescent and vanishing. I know that sometimes swimmers count their strokes as a measure; keeping an exact count of every reach is a meditative exercise much like the Buddhist practice of *kinhin*, a walking contemplation in which they walk clockwise around a room, timing each step with each breath. While such discipline has always seemed extreme to me, I understand now that there is something universal about the desire to calculate experience by attending to its smallest increments.

From the height of the bridge, the Hudson is an endless river, so wide with possibility that one could forgive Henry Hudson for believing it the route to China. It is a view that speaks not only to the continuum of flowing water and the distance it has traveled, but to the continuum of time; and when confronted with these from the middle of that bridge, it is easy to believe that both of them are limitless. Whenever I cross that bridge from the west, I know I have reached home: I enter the Hudson Valley well to the west of the bridge, somewhere in the foothills of the Catskill Mountains. The ridgeline of the Catskills, the particulars of the clouds over the mountains, the oak and maple woodlands, all of these signal home, but most of all, of course, it is the river. On lesser journeys, that realization isn't significant, but on longer trips the bridge is always its own destination. I remember once coming to that bridge after five days of driving from San Francisco to my family's house in the Hudson Valley, and the sense of relief I felt on seeing the river. Although there were another twenty miles before I reached the house, its hedge of peonies, maple trees, and three apple trees, the bridge was the landmark that announced most clearly that I had arrived.

Crossing the river in the water itself, some fifty feet below the bridge, underscored that sense of arrival. Labor Day has always been a landmark of apprehension and dread in my own interior calendar, much the way New Year's is for many; it signals a coming bleakness, that time when days get noticeably shorter, the air cools, and the first of the seven long, dark months until March creeps in. Coming at this day from the water helped; it confirmed the sense of passage.

From the top of Beacon Mountain on its eastern bank, this stretch of the river is a different landscape altogether. Andrew Jackson Downing, one of America's preeminent landscape designers of the nineteenth century, hiked the Hudson Highlands as a boy, and of the view from the summit of the mountain he wrote: "The Hudson—the prince of rivers! It appears to you that you see it rising like a silvery rivulet, thirty miles north of you in those distant hills, gradually widening, meandering, spreading life and freshness around, until here it loses itself, a deep, broad, powerful current in the rent chasms of the highlands." His description holds true 170 years later. The rocky summit of Beacon Mountain marks a point of transition in the topography of the valley, and the route of our swim also marked a place where the character of the river changes decisively. To the north, the reach of the river is a shimmering silver corridor that winds quietly through the rolling hills of the valley up through Dutchess, Ulster, and Columbia counties. Downriver, though, the river cuts a more dramatic path through the Appalachian ridge; glaciers carving their way through to the sea during the Ice Age Sliced a passage through the granite. On the west side of the river, Storm King Mountain serves as the gateway to the Hudson Highlands, and it is a place where the river meets the definition of a fjord; mountains of granite and limestone drop sharply into the narrow and deep channel; the river is deeper here than anywhere else, some two hundred feet to the bottom. A view of that Hudson conjures both startling geologic cataclysm along with a sense of great repose; oddly, the image of water cutting through rock evokes a sense of stillness.

But that is the view from the mountain. My impressions midriver, when fully immersed in the opaque, gray waves, were different still. Although we had seemed to jump into the river quickly and more or less together, we had scattered afar by the time we reached midriver. The wind, the current, and our varying senses of direction all worked to separate us, and each swimmer seemed suddenly solitary. From the little whitecap I was caught up in, the sense of time and water stretching endlessly on either side was replaced by a perspective of immediacy. Caught up in these whitecaps, I had the sensation of being in a small, even confined space. Perhaps it is a human impulse to construct borders and margins for ourselves when the world around us seems too spacious; maybe it is only natural to devise a small intimate space when nature seems so boundless. Here it was a random and improvisational arrangement, a fluid little room defined by whitecaps in the middle of the river that answered to a desire to feel close and contained.

One doesn't feel this intimacy with the natural world often. Maybe it is simply because the body is 70 percent water, but it is easy to imagine yourself to be a particle in the river's—and even nature's—continuity. That continuity is reassuring. You somehow go through life to a certain point always thinking that even if you can't exactly start over, at least you can fix things or change them and that all the missteps and wrong directions can be corrected and that it is never too late. Later, you may find yourself believing that is no longer true. I looked up the river and down it. Its flow was certain, its direction unchangeable, but still it could take on the day's nuances of light, the vagaries of the shifting tide.

Despite being separated by the whitecaps, by the current, and each by our own often deviant sense of direction, a sense of community prevailed. That happened especially with parents who were swimming with their kids; not surprisingly, the notion of swimming across a wide river can tap into a parent's most primal fears. At one point midriver, I found myself listening to the strains of "I Could Have Danced All Night." Mary Arnold and her thirteen-year-old daughter were singing show tunes to keep themselves motivated. "My daughter was born a mermaid," Arnold told me later. She had been classically trained and sings professionally, and although I had not expected to encounter magical realism that day on the Hudson, the songs from *The King and I* and *My Fair Lady* echoing across the river did not seem out of place. The premise of musical theater is that when the spoken word is insufficient expression, one breaks into song, and certainly such an impulse of dramatic exultation was understandable that afternoon. Besides, such tunes as "Shall We Dance" and "I Could Have Danced All Night" suggested the image of the riverbed as a dance floor, which wasn't much of a stretch; certainly there was a sense of ceremony, and if dance is sometimes a way of finding a new movement, a new step, crossing new ground, the swim qualified as all of those. Moreover, the waltz, the foxtrot, the Charleston, and the breast stroke, the butterfly, the crawl, all are a system of ordering human movement with both grace and efficiency; all of them a repetition of rhythmic gestures that are at once precise and fluid. Arnold herself put it more simply. Explaining her notion of swimming as a social experience, she later told me, "I guess I always took to heart the admonition 'always swim with a buddy.' "

Mihaly Csikszentmihalyi is a professor and former chairman of the psychology department at the University of Chicago, and the author of flow theory. This theory might as well be about swimming because it proposes that human experience is fullest when it is the result of action and awareness converging; when this happens—whether through play, sport, ritual, pageantry, or some other activity—consciousness becomes ordered and experience pleasurable and sustaining. In *Flow: The Psychology of Optimal Experience*, he writes that "flow tends to integrate the self because in that state of deep concentration, consciousness is unusually well ordered. Thoughts, intentions, feelings, and all the senses are focused on the same goal. Experience is in harmony." While Sprawson's lonely and delusional swimmer might not see it this way, such convictions of a well-ordered consciousness sounded to me like as good a way as any to describe the pleasures of swimming across a river.

Meta had her own way of articulating flow theory. "It was the first time I had ever swum in the Hudson," she told me later. "But I had heard about people swimming in the river, and it was massively important that I do this swim. The water tasted incredibly soft and sweet. I had expected it to taste a little salty, but it wasn't. It just had a sweetness. And I knew then that river water is not to be compared to any swimming pool I had ever been in. And there was also just this incredible expanse. You could really stretch out; you could really be a part of it. It was the equivalent of running across a huge meadow. You have this huge expanse, and that you are immersed in it is the key

thing. And the idea that you could be able to offer that to other people, and to people all around the country, that would be an incredible experience. It completely remotivated me." Her words evoked
Chillemi's assurance to his swimmers that they would take ownership of the river. But they also suggested that it is a fluid exchange.
The real estate of the water flows through your hands, and the river
owns a bit of you. Intimacy with the river, like other kinds of intimacy, is laced with ambiguity, with questions of ownership elusive
and variable.

As we passed the halfway point across the river, traffic on the
western side was gradually allowed to resume. A barge that had
paused upriver now picked up speed, and its wake sent another sequence of choppy waves in our direction, and that, along with the
suddenly strengthening tide, gave the river a new force. The swim
had been timed to begin half an hour before slack tide, but conditions at sea can affect the timing of the current and tides, and earlier
in the week, the weather had been stormy. Despite the efforts and intentions of the organizers, the tide was now coming in earlier than
expected, creating a strong upriver current, and swimming the last
several hundred feet downstream to the Beacon marina suddenly
became labored. Established river lore has it that due to the ever-
alternating directions of tide and current, a stick thrown into the
Hudson at Troy will not reach New York City until a year and a half
later. I can't speak to the accuracy of this, yet the beginning pull of
the tide made it seem possible; this is a river that can pull you every
which way. Our swim across the Hudson three years earlier had
taken place on a tranquil day at a narrower stretch of river just a few
miles north; swimming the river that day was akin to swimming in a
calm lake. The river was wider here, though, and the added distance
and time introduced me to a stronger and more capricious body of
water. Growing up in the Hudson Valley, I had never swum in the
river. Both the pollution of the river and its perceived strength had

put it beyond reach. Now I had swum in the river twice, and it had been entirely different each time. I wondered if it would be relegated to that realm of experience—people or facts—about which the more you learn the less you know.

Ordinarily, the sensation of being overwhelmed or overpowered is likely to come during some kind of hardship, at the death or loss of someone you love or catastrophic natural disaster, and it is possible to imagine that your identity has been consumed by external forces, and your spirit is in havoc. I remember swimming once with my son Luc, then about ten, in the Atlantic Ocean off Fire Island. We had swum out past the surf and were bobbing in the waves, drifting toward danger without knowing it. Minutes later, watching the shoreline recede, I realized that we were caught in a riptide. Holding on to him with one hand, I waved frantically to our friends on the shore, but they only waved back, thinking we were simply exulting in our afternoon swim; how strange that our gestures for terror and joy should be so similar as to be mistaken for each other. Near panic then, I grabbed his hand tighter and paddled with the other hand down the surf until we caught a wave that returned us to shore.

Swimming in the river that afternoon was some sibling sensation of that experience, but if the flow of the river was overpowering, the loss of identity was sustaining. Swimming in a river—rather than a pond or pool or lake—answers to the part of you that *wants* to be swept away. Maybe that's why it's a way to right yourself. Maybe this is the lesson that arrived in the current of the Delaware River, that ran downstream the Connecticut, that flowed through the Susquehanna as well, and that now was reflected in the Hudson River a second time. "When I was home I dreamed of the river, but on the river I dreamed of home," wrote William Least Heat-Moon on his cross-country river trip, and it is a sentiment now familiar to me; those two parts of my life lean on each other. And if from time to time I step off and away from that familiar scaffolding of family and profession that I have attached my life to, getting lost in the stream of a river seems a safe bet; you can't leave your footprints on a river. Besides, it's a more reasonable choice than other more conventional modes of stepping outside the framework. In that way the natural world has of so often reaching us in some unpredictable and astonishing way, all of these rivers have conferred a kind of fluid axis that sets me right every time.

The flotilla of kayaks on either side of the swimmers guided us to the shore, where we were met with a banquet of roasted corn on the cob, sweet potato pie, and chocolate coconut energy bars, a hybrid menu of soul food and engineered nutrition. We didn't all reach the shore at the same time, not even close. I later learned that the fastest swimmer had made it in about twenty minutes. It took me closer to forty-five. But the measure of equality has never been an exact science. Meta mused that the drawing of the pool "looks a little like a petrie dish," and it seemed like an apt image, because what seemed to be germinating most robustly was Seeger's sought-after community allegiance to the river. It was clear by then that if damage arrives collectively, so too does recovery.

Certainly the degradation of the Hudson River has come through an assortment of collective enterprises: unchecked industrial abuse from a consortium of pulp mills and paper factories, tanneries, auto plants, utilities companies, and power plants, much of which residue remains embedded in the river. And while there has been little raw sewage flowing into the river since the mid-eighties, the greater threat today is the nonpoint pollution, such as agricultural fertilizers, pesticides, and road salt. Even the biological pollutants arrive en masse in an improvisational conspiracy. The water chestnuts that arrived in the late 1800s as ornamental species from Europe today spread their city of leaves across the surface of the water, their wide canopy preventing light from infiltrating the surface, and stopping anything from growing there. Their long tufted stems further choke the river, deoxygenating the water and starving the aquatic life beneath its surface. The zebra mussels arrived in the early nineties by taking up residence in the ballast water of transoceanic cargo ships. By consuming microscopic plant and animals at the base of the food chain, their colonies have managed to devour the nutrients needed by other aquatic species, throwing into chaos the balance of the river's ecosystem. In the same way the contours of the Delaware River were reshaped as an accident of deforestation, the transformation of this river is the result of nothing more than negligence. Dr. David L. Strayer, an aquatic ecologist at the Institute of Ecosystem Studies, underscores the fact that the way in which the zebra mussels have changed the entire character of the Hudson River was not the result of conscious action. "We just let it happen through our carelessness," he says.

But if devastation visits the river in one communal enterprise after the other, a parallel sense of collectivity may reclaim it. In 2006 a group of thirty-five hundred swimmers crossed the Pearl River in Guangzhou in southern China to raise awareness of pollution, metal concentrations in the sediment, lead and cadmium especially. The swimmers, it was reported, could not see their own feet in the murky water; the number of swimmers seems commensurate to the degree of restoration required. After the group swim across the Hudson, I looked back out on the river and then to the site where the river pool will eventually be installed. Zollner had said earlier that one of the biggest obstacles to swimming in rivers is psychological, because of their history of pollution, and the celebratory atmosphere of the afternoon made some preliminary assault on that conviction. To the poet Algernon Charles Swinburne, swimming was a way to regain a paradise lost; in his poem "A Swimmer's Dream" he speaks of "a peace more happy than lives on land." The kayaks had been hauled up onto the shore, and they announced themselves as some kind of list of accessories for deliverance: *Aquafusion*, *Perception*, *Heritage*, *In-nova*, *Liquidlogic*, *Epic*, *Current*. I imagined these not just as the seemingly frail vessels that had shepherded us across the river, but as reflecting some larger collective force that will help to redeem this river.

There was nothing clear about the river here. This was not a clear running stream but a wide torrent of turbid gray water, and its very lack of clarity posed problems for the river pool; to be deep enough for adults to swim in, a minimum of eight or nine feet, the bottom needs to remain visible. Possibly, the pool could be filled from the top with a layer of clear water that is continually circulated to its lower depths. Or some kind of filtering material might be used to control turbidity. Or possibly the bottom of the pool could be redesigned to be raised or lowered as the river turbidity varies. Meta is certain there is a design solution to this, and maybe it's her conviction, or Zollner's pragmatism, or Seeger's vision, or a combination of all of these, but I have no doubt that someday there will be a pool full of clear water at the edge of this river.

In her formal description of the river pool, Meta wrote that "the hybrid character of this project, being neither pool, boat, building or beach and yet combining aspects of all the above, creates an example of a structure that blurs the boundaries between inside and outside, figure and ground, creating a new kind of programmatic interaction between people and the aquatic environment." Seeger put it differently. Throughout the summer months, public lakes and ponds in the state may be closed by the Department of Health if water turbidity hinders lifeguards' underwater vision. "But beaches don't have to close," he told me after the swim. "I say this is not a pool but a swimming net. This is a nomenclature thing. This is a floating beach, if anyone asks." That ambiguity may be essential to what's going on. Whether it is in a petrie dish or a river pool, many things begin with this lack of clarity, with little idea of what you are starting with or where you will end up or whether it is a beach or a pool, a boat or a building, inside or out.

It is a common paradox that the people who least assume the mantle of self-assurance often have it the most. Maybe it's nothing more than a kind of highly evolved buddy system, but something that has always set Seeger apart is his relentless tenacity in attributing the credit for his work to others. Reminiscing about his songwriting, he once told a radio interviewer, "I wrote the song, but the reason it became so well known is because of all the other singers and musicians who made it great." And of his work with the *Clearwater*, he once told a journalist, "I got more credit than I deserve for starting it, but I didn't know what I was doing, and the people who deserve the credit are the people who have sat in the office and wrassled with budgets and somehow managed to raise the money year after year." So I wasn't surprised that when I bumped into Seeger a month or so after the swim and we started to talk about the swim, after congratulating me on making it, he said, "Now I must ask you first to be critical, to tell us how we can make it better next year." We talked about the tides and the timing, and he reiterated his hope that on some swim, someday, "everyone will reach the shore at the same time." And then he congratulated me again and said, "It's you people who are going to change the way the public thinks of the river." I knew by then he meant that as a challenge.

I thought of Dennis Chillemi's embarrassment when he was asked if he felt that he had inspired his group of swimmers. Though of a different generation, character, and occupation, he echoed Seeger. "I don't look at it that way," he said. "It's a work in progress. It's part of my life. Now if we could find a cure for MS, then that would be an achievement." The Hudson River being the natural habitat for both men, it seems possible that their egos have long since been diluted by the current. I read in *Flow* that "the loss of the sense of self separate from the world around it is sometimes accompanied by a feeling of union with the environment." Certainly these words could be a direct reference to both of these men, and I wonder whether that's the trick. Solitude may be nothing more than some oblique strategy for self-assertion, nothing more than its own form of self-interest. Perhaps it is a different kind of obscurity I am after, the kind of obscurity I caught a glimpse of earlier that day on the pier when none of us at the edge of the river seemed given to rating ourselves or our abilities, that kind of anonymity that can be found in a crowd, in the current of a fast-flowing river, in a larger sense of purpose, or in a greater recognition of humanity. My sons would know how to put this more simply. "Just get over yourself," they would say.

It doesn't always take a river to get over yourself, but it's a good place to start. And if I rely on the largesse of the river world to sweep me away every now and then, I know as well that a similar largesse of human effort may be what it takes to reclaim the Hudson River. It is unlikely to be any lone gesture or solitary act or single piece of legislation, but rather that brand of work that only has meaning when people work through each other. If I can manage to take any small extract of this water with me today, it will be this: Just as much as this river is a border and a divide, its current and its flow and its tide can all be used to connect.

It was the end of the afternoon by then, and the crowd was thinning out. The swimmers were dressed, the kayakers had loaded their kayaks back onto their trucks, and the musicians playing from the back of a pickup had packed up. Close to ten thousand dollars had been raised. Seeger was on the old wooden pier where earlier, he and sloop club members had leaned several aluminum ladders in the river, so the swimmers would have river egress. Installing the ladders is a job Seeger cherishes; they have to be tied to the dock just so, with a particular knot that allows the ladders to accommodate the rise and fall of the river. Now he took them out of the water and laid them, one by one, on the ground nearby. It was the assured gesture of a river steward who knew that the swim, and summer, were over. It was also a gesture that invited one to imagine a season or two hence when river access will not be an improvisational arrangement of aluminum ladders but a more reliable and gracious construction that reconnects communities and the people in them with the river running through them.

The Monongahela and Cheat Rivers

POINT MARION, PENNSYLVANIA

MAY 21, 2005

IT HAD RAINED the day before, but by the time I got into Point Marion, the skies had cleared, and it had even begun to feel like an early summer morning. The spring had been unusually cool; after a run of warm days in April that had promised respite from winter, the temperature had again dropped, and it wasn't until early June that warm summer days actually arrived in the Northeast. Since swimming in the Hudson River nearly nine months earlier, I had been swimming indoors. I was anxious now to be in running water, and I had planned my swim for late May knowing the river would still be running with the chill of winter. But the drive to Point Marion seemed to deliver me directly to summer. I was in a different climate zone from that of the Hudson Valley, and the air felt as though it were on the cusp of the new season; banks of wild purple phlox clustered along the roadside, along with hedges of wild daisies and smatterings of poppies. As I drove into town, irises, azaleas, and huge bursts of rhododendron were in full bloom.

On my way to Point Marion, I had stopped to see my friend Barbara Flanagan in Bethlehem. I was traveling alone on this trip. Onni was still in school, and I had decided to go ahead without her. So when Barbara gave me the small medal for my protection, I was happy to have it. "Here," she had said, handing me a little round refrigerator magnet. "You can have it. I got it from the man who sells me fish. It's Saint Antonio. He'll watch over you during your swim." Having spent three years studying with the nuns at the Convent of the Sacred Heart when I was in elementary school, I knew what I was looking at was a Saint Christopher medal. Etched on its surface was the familiar design of the patron saint of travelers, a bearded man with a staff, fording a stream and carrying on his back a small child with a radiant little halo around his head; often I would go to school with just such a medal pinned to the collar of my white Peter Pan blouse. This was a saint I *knew*. Saint Antonio, so far as I could recall, had something to do with protecting the animals in the stable, and he was sometimes pictured with a large pink pig, nowhere in evidence on the medal I was holding. Barbara had been raised as a Catholic but had converted to Judaism. I had been raised as an Episcopalian but had gone to Catholic school, and clearly it was going to take the two of us, with our mixed bag of spiritual education, to sort out the matters of the man and the child and the pig. But we muddled through, and I felt heartened by the fact that she had given me the saint I had needed without ever knowing his name. And it made sense. How we manage to take care of ourselves is often a matter of blind luck, a process of strange and unexpected happenstance. Along with all the signs of summer outside the car window, the little trinket on the dashboard made me feel that things were right with the world.

Which I had not expected. The Monongahela River begins in

the streams of the Allegheny Mountains and is formed by the confluence of the West Fork and Tygart rivers in Fairmont, West Virginia. It flows north from there for 128 miles to Pittsburgh, where it converges with the Allegheny River to form the Ohio River. We intuitively think of upriver as a northerly direction, downriver as south, north as going against the current, south as going with it. Linguistically, physically, and geographically, a river that flows north seems to defy the logic of the natural world. But the flow of water doesn't conform to the points of the compass. Rather than observing longitude and latitude, it is governed by altitude alone. Rivers flow from high places to low places, and they flow in only one direction, which is down. We are likely to believe that rivers flow south because that's what rivers generally do; in most cases, the mountain source of the river *is* to the north of its mouth. Yet the 4,150-mile-long Nile is an exception, as is the seventy-eight-mile-long Eel River in California.

And the Monongahela. It is only human to feel curious about things when they are not as we think they are meant to be. I had expected that its northerly flow would somehow contradict the current of blood in my own veins, reading as physically and geographically incorrect; and that in relation to the path the sun takes across the sky and one's innate physical awareness of the points of the compass, the direction of its current would somehow feel instinctively inaccurate. And if rivers are the key arteries in my own system of cognitive mapping, it had seemed important to cross this river that flowed the wrong way. Like a hailstorm in July or the summer sky darkening in a solar eclipse, I'd imagined not chaos so much as a small incident of anarchy in the natural world, a defeat of intuition. I had come here hoping to be confronted by such a seeming misalignment as a river that flows to the north, and the affirmation that if the natural world can accommodate *that*, surely it could also accommodate my own lesser misalliances, errors of judgment, impulsive words and gestures.

Actually, I had arrived at Point Marion almost by default. As with so many other rivers, swimming access had been difficult to determine from a distance, in this case five hundred miles, so I had resorted to calling the Army Corps of Engineers, which operates the system of locks and dams along the river. What I had heard from the corps were the usual mixed messages; by then, I had become accustomed to the attitude of studied ambivalence and had even become a little heartened by the sheer familiarity of it all. The engineer I talked to at Lock Three, for example, wasn't discouraging in any overt way, but he had outlined the concerns. "From Morgantown to Pittsburgh there is a fair amount of commercial traffic. Go upriver to Point Marion," he had advised. It's also a lot cleaner there, with less industrial waste, and less chance of sewage overflow. "But personally," he had added, "I wouldn't do it." When we had spoken earlier in the month, the water temperature had only been in the mid-fifties, and while he hadn't made any overt effort to dissuade me, he was guarded, circumspect at best. But then the last thing he said to me before we got off the phone was "Good luck to you." I recognized him to be a member of that community of people whose allegiance to the river prevents them from wholly disparaging the enterprise. And as I continued to work my way down the lock system, talking to assorted engineers and operators at the corps, they had all pretty much told me the same things: Sure, you can swim in the river. It's a little dirty, but it's not very wide, and it's not very strong. But you just wouldn't want to do it here. Point Marion, I had heard repeatedly, is where you want to go. And good luck.

A small town of 1,200 in southwestern Pennsylvania, Port Marion is just a few miles from the West Virginia border. It's in the heart of Pennsylvania coal country, and there are still numerous active mines in the area, both underground and surface. The river has long been the essential commercial artery for the steel and coal industries, but with the steel belt long giving way to the rust belt, it came as no surprise to find a community down on its luck. As I drove by looking for the community park that fronts on the river, I saw a teenage boy trolling the plot of bare earth in front of his house with a metal detector, that accessory universally cherished by the displaced. While the more well-to-do community is situated on the hill above the river, the riverfront conveyed all the mixed messages of so many American river communities. Without a doubt it has remained a landscape of industry. A behemoth glass plant at the southern edge of town, the Houze Glass Corporation, manufactured ceramic mugs, beer steins, and the like, but it had closed six months earlier after 102 years, and a sign out front announced an auction for real estate and equipment the following week. A century ago, there were seven glass factories in the area, but the Houze was the last to shut down operations, a result of outsourcing and moving the remainder of its operations to a facility in Texas. Just south of the glass factory is the Point Marion Locks and Dam, and just below that, the Fort Martin Power Plant. Small wonder that riverfront property has rarely been regarded as desirable; many of the residences along the river read as old tenant housing in disrepair.

The population had fallen by several hundred, and the school closed over a decade ago; the building now serves as a nursing home. And when I found it, even the community park at the riverfront conveyed its own sense of ambiguity; river reclamation has been going on here for generations, it seems, though much of it has been thwarted. The picnic pavilions, corrugated metal roofs resting on steel supports in a kind of aspirational wing formation, could have been built in the sixties when public works looked with hope to the idioms of modern design, while the yellow plastic slides of the playground are clearly more recent. But there were a couple of tennis courts, overgrown with weeds, that looked like they hadn't been used in years. The result seemed to be the commonplace combination of a failure in public funds and a lack of conviction in the people that the river is someplace you might want to be. Still, the park itself was maintained, the grass mowed, and in the evening, kids were playing in the ball-park. Nothing in the park keeps you from the river, but all the same, activities don't seem much oriented toward it. It's as though people want to use the river, but just how they might do that has never quite been worked out.

After all, I considered, the Monongahela is a place of work, not play, and that the river is a primarily industrial artery is underscored quickly. I'd been at the park only a few minutes before I saw a tug, the *R. L. Ireland*, owned by the Consolidated Coal Company, go by, pushing three barges loaded with coal to the power plant. That it was going south, upriver, still seemed strange to me. Directly up the river are the locks and dam. In its natural state, the Monongahela is too shallow for navigation, and starting in the mid-nineteenth century, a series of locks and dams were constructed to maintain a constant, navigable water level, enabling barges to transport millions of tons of coal that would generate the energy for the steel mills in Pittsburgh and power plants along the Ohio River.

I had arranged to meet Dennis and Marcia Groce at the community park. A few weeks earlier, a Point Marion borough council member whose name I had come across online had listened patiently on the telephone while I explained my hope to swim in the Mon— along with my hope of finding someone to spot me in a canoe or kayak. When I had finished, without missing a beat, he had just said, "You ought to call Dennis Groce. He might be interested." I did, and he was. If my search for river access had been met with ambivalence by the Army Corps of Engineers, the Groces made up for that; they directed me to Web sites that monitor water temperature, offered me a wet suit, dinner, a spare room to sleep in. So when they finally drove into the parking lot with a canoe strapped to the rack on the roof of the car, I knew that I was in the company of compatriots. A semiretired engineer with NIOSH, the National Institute for Occupational Safety and Health, Dennis may view the world with the exacting eye of a scientist, but he also conveys an immediate and palpable affection for the landscape around him, whether it is the river or the rolling hills, so many of them scarred by mining, just beyond.

"Should be a great day," he had written in his last e-mail to me, and when they put their canoe in the water, they seemed genuinely pleased to be there, operating with the faith that the river is where a person of sound mind would likely choose to be on a sunny morning in May. My sense of gratitude to them was tempered only slightly by the suspicion that it actually doesn't take much to get these two out on the river. Directly across the river from where I was standing was a large sign that said ARRIVAL POINT. It is meant to signal the tugs and barges approaching the locks, but I was content that morning to interpret it more personally.

Getting into the water required stepping around a truck, trailer, and the recently poured concrete of the new boat launch, which for the moment was covered with sheets of plastic. Stepping through a miniconstruction site to get to the water isn't something you'd ordinarily want to do, but this new launch seemed so full of hope for the riverfront that I was happy to be there; it was a launch in every sense of the word. Financed by a one-hundred-thousand-dollar grant from the Pennsylvania Fish and Boat Commission, it was a first step toward using the river for the town's economic recovery. Once completed, the dock would be able to accommodate not only kayaks and canoes but much larger motorized boats as well. It was designed to be a stop along the Monongahela Water Trail, a trail for boaters that runs from Fairmont, West Virginia, to Pittsburgh. If the new launch could make Point Marion an enticing stop for boaters, who could tie up there and go into the shops and restaurants in town, it would be a small but significant step toward the town's revitalization.

The river was an opaque muddy green from the rains of the previous day, and it was still cool, somewhere in the low sixties. And although it was only a hundred yards or so wide, after swimming in a pool for so many months, I found that its chill, its opacity, and its quiet current all made for more water than I had been in all winter. It has a density and a substance to it. I know that in ordinary circumstances, clarity is something to value—in words, in thought, in expression, in behavior. I have never found any reason to argue with W. H. Auden's statement that great art is simply clear thinking about mixed feelings.

Yet on this particular May morning in the middle of the Monongahela River, it was the absence of clarity that gave the water its character. It was living and real and genuine, and it was full of mystery and obscurity, and its identity seemed derived from its very lack of transparency. The water came from some other place and time; the fact that it had traveled the distance from a ridge of mountains in a different state, that it was flowing with the chill of an earlier season, and that it had taken its own time to do so all suggested that it had a brief history of its own, and it was difficult to believe that it shared its name with the anemic, antiseptic substance I had been swimming in all winter. That morning the river water even had a kind of loamy taste to it, almost an earthen flavor. The name of the river translates to "river of falling banks," and the crumbling earth of its banks is in the nature of the river, a characteristic that is underscored after a rain when the water has even more sediment than usual.

The fact that it was a Saturday morning hadn't done much to slow the commercial traffic on the river, and only minutes earlier we had watched another tug push a barge upriver toward the power plant. I swam out to a green channel marker about a third of the way across, but nothing was coming so I just kept swimming to the other side to a thicket of river birches, maple, willows, and cottonwoods. The current pulled, but there wasn't much to it, and if I had been expecting its northern flow to feel off, I couldn't have been more mistaken. The dam had opened three of its floodgates that morning to release water from the rains of the day before; nonetheless, the current was just a subdued, steady pull. I realized I was listening for the barges on their way to the power plant, but what I heard most clearly was the shrill hum of cars passing over the steel grate of the bridge just downstream to the north.

Going south upriver continues to sound all wrong, as does going downstream to the north. But the river itself was oblivious to my anticipation, as is so often the case in our relations with the natural world. It is only the language that is off base; there was nothing about the river or the morning that was out of order. If being swept by the current of the Hudson down toward the ocean had provided a certain thrill and exhilaration, I anticipated that the pull of a north-flowing current would bring on an even greater expression of astonishment. But nothing like this happened, of course, and I realized my expectation had all the logic of thinking you can plan for the unexpected.

Besides, there is a certain inevitability about rivers; they just go where they are going to go, and it's not bad to be reminded of this. Things happen; you do what needs to be done; life goes on—clichés, all of them, to be sure, but they are still steady reminders of how continuity is a simple life force. Sometimes, it is the most you can ask for. When one of Carl Jung's patients solicited his advice on what she should do with her life, Jung answered, "Do the most necessary thing." The most necessary thing, I know, can range from the frivolous to the serious; there are days it might mean planting bulbs or making a pot of soup and days when it might mean sitting quietly alone in a room and days when it might mean finding a new job or scheduling surgery. It is a deceptively simple directive, not nearly so easy as it sounds. It has three parts: You have to know what the most necessary thing is; then you have to will yourself to do it; and then you do it. But it seems to me that a river, especially one that is running high with spring rain and flowing north, is that feature in nature that embodies most precisely doing the most necessary thing. The most necessary thing at that particular moment for me is just to swim back to the other side.

As I was standing on the edge of the river, Dennis said, "Come on, so long as you're still wet, you may as well swim across the Cheat. Marcia and I will paddle over, you'll drive there, and we'll meet by the shore," and then they were gone. I was fortunate, I realized, to have found them. When I had first spoken to Dennis on the phone from New York, he had understood the impulse to swim the river almost immediately and within minutes was suggesting locations for the swim. Or swims, as it turned out. After telling me about the easy access point at the community park in town, he had also suggested a spot just a mile or so up the river where the Mason-Dixon Line crosses the river. Also the state line between Pennsylvania and West Virginia, it crosses the river on a quiet stretch between the plant and the dam, and the steady flow of the current underscores the river's indifference to property lines, political boundaries, and human demarcations of any sort. "But there's the Cheat River, too," he had told me. "Point Marion is at the confluence of the Cheat and Monongahela rivers, and you could swim the Cheat at the place where George Washington crossed the river in 1784." And suddenly, to swim in two rivers that flow north in one day seemed like an extravagance of fortune.

Maybe it's in the nature of being an activist, but there is a generosity of spirit in Dennis and Marcia. Whether it is volunteering in the local library, mentoring schoolkids, being actively engaged in the local Lutheran church, or organizing public information meetings about the construction of a new power plant, they both seem instinctively committed to community advocacy. That there are many rivers to cross is something they easily accept; they understand that if it's geographically feasible, swimming across two rivers is always preferable to swimming across one. And I have little doubt that had there been a third or fourth river in proximity, Dennis would have said with equal parts nonchalance and conviction, "Well, come on, while we're at it, we may as well do these."

I know by now there is no vocabulary that is exclusive to saving rivers. Why would there be? But when scientists and environmentalists speak of what has happened to American rivers, they use words like *impair*, *degrade*, *suffer*, and *abuse*, words of human pain often at the hands of other humans. It is not so much that we are anthropomorphizing these geographic entities, but more, perhaps, that we recognize them in us and us in them. Perhaps this is why the activists I meet on riverfronts are so deeply and proudly and emotionally engaged with the waters around them. And so without much more discussion, I drove to the parking lot of the Point Marion firehouse, where an old, rusted-out staircase leads down through a bank thick with weeds to the Cheat River.

The river begins in the West Virginia mountains some 157 miles to the south, and its narrows, gorges, and numerous rapids have long made it a supreme kayaking and boating waterway. If the Monongahela was running with mud and sediment that morning, partially on account of the rains the day before, the Cheat, in comparison, looked to be a clear stream. The diverse character of the two rivers is spelled out at their confluence. I was swimming just feet above the place where the rivers meet, and the demarcation line remained explicit; the two paths of water met, remained separate, flowed north in parallel streams. If the silt and sediment of the Monongahela have given it an opaque brown hue, the Cheat was an unexpectedly clear green, due in part to its higher pH factor. In his *Theory of Colours*, the German writer Goethe said of the color green: "If yellow and blue, which we consider as the most fundamental and simple colours, are united as they first appear, in the first state of their action, the colour which we call green is the result. The eye experiences a distinctly grateful impression from this colour. If the two elementary colours are mixed in perfect equality, so that neither predominates, the eye and mind repose on the result of this junction as upon a simple colour. The beholder has neither the wish nor the power to imagine a state beyond it." That was about how green the Cheat was that morning.

Artists and painters and anyone else who has ever worked with color knows that hues are brought out with all the more intensity when they are juxtaposed with another color, and some similar principle may have been at work here that morning. Or perhaps it wasn't in the science of color and light waves; I don't think there is anything really in a milky brown that makes green all that more intense, yet the vibrance of each river seemed accentuated by its proximity to the other. Maybe it wasn't so much the chemistry of color and pigment, but more of personality and character, the way one of two partners or friends or siblings can sometimes bring out the truest and best self of the other.

Just a couple of miles upstream from the confluence of the two rivers is Cheat Lake, created by the construction of Lake Lynn Hydro Station Dam in 1925. I had passed the dam the day before while coming into town and had noticed the public warning system for the first mile below it. An elaborate and dramatic system of flashing yellow and red lights along with loudspeakers with prerecorded announcements is in place to warn people about sudden and unexpected changes in the water level; it had been hard to miss the huge red and white warning signs along the riverfront announcing, WATER LEVEL THROUGH PLANT IS AUTOMATICALLY CONTROLLED AND CAN GO TO MAXIMUM VERY QUICKLY FROM HERE TO DAM. Moments earlier I had pulled my car off to the side of the road to see if I could gauge the width of the river and its velocity. Still, when suddenly activated in the woodlands along the river, the flashing red lights seemed out of place. The voice on the speakers was loud and garbled, and although the words were incomprehensible, I had stepped back reflexively, then waited, watching for the sudden flood of water or rise in level. If I had been expecting some biblical change in the scenery, it was only because the warning system invited such dire conjecture. But, in fact, nothing much had seemed to happen; the river continued to flow, more or less unchanged.

The waters of the Cheat are stronger too. Midstream, I realized it makes sense that a river is called a body of water. It is a body with a sinew and strength of its own; its currents are dark, they offer little visibility, they are not easily known. Images of the warning system upriver revisited me, and I wondered if I had been foolishly cavalier in not determining what water releases were to be made that morning. Even the name of the river is layered with meanings that revisited me midriver. Possibly, it is a reference to the darkness of its waters that can deceive one's vision. Others attribute it to the series of rapids upstream that are today looked upon as challenging to whitewater boaters and that have presumably cheated numerous lives over the years. Possibly, too, it was derived from the name of a French Huguenot who settled the area in the early 1700s, Jacques Cheathe.

But the meaning I chose to believe in that morning was the name that reflected the unpredictable nature of the river. Changeability is in the character of the Cheat. The steep slopes of its bank upstream allow lower sections of the lower river to flood unexpectedly; and as in other rivers that flow from mountainous regions, the water level of the Cheat can change quickly, up to six or eight inches in an hour; while it could be a placid, sunny day downstream, the river might rise quickly and unexpectedly from runoff caused by rain at its headlands, sweeping away whatever was left on the banks. That the Cheat is inhospitable to swimmers is not an uncommon view and is one that has historic precedence. For the towns built along the river, the possibility of rising waters is ever present, and they are perpetually vulnerable to flooding; among the people who live in these communities, the folklore is that the river will kill you.

Midriver, the current came on suddenly, and then, just as unexpectedly, was stilled. The force of the river threads its waters erratically;

the Cheat isn't a wide river, but it still seems to accommodate all the unpredictability of a grander, stronger river. There is a sandbar just a short ways upstream, and for some seventy-five years, the Mclain Sand Company mined the sand of the Cheat for construction materials for local industry. Today, the remnants of that operation still mark the river, rusted steel artifacts emerging from the water's surface, antique witnesses to the river's industrial lineage. Immediately upstream are the vestiges of stonework from an old highway bridge and the concrete piers from a railroad bridge, both now gone. I was aiming to reach one of the bridge abutments, but the current would have nothing to do with that, and I found myself fifteen or twenty feet below them by the time I reached the other side. "Am I swimming in place?" I asked Marsha and Dennis nearby in the canoe. "Not quite," Dennis said, but with little conviction, and I wasn't convinced myself until I suddenly found myself in more quiet water. I treaded water for a minute or two, not anxious to be out just yet.

Weeks later, I had occasion to put questions about the Cheat's current to Duane Nichols. A retired chemical engineer, he is one of the river's many stewards, and the head of the Cheat Lake Environment and Recreational Association (CLEAR), and he pointed out that what happens when water is released from the dam is barely visible. The change in flow is discernible in more subtle ways, not as a sudden wall of water but as a gradual increase in pressure that you might notice if, for example, you stood with a stick in the water for twenty minutes. He told me that while the acid mine drainage doesn't pose much of a risk for swimmers, they are at risk from boulders, from wild vines of poison ivy and poison oak, and from snakes. "Rattlesnakes are rare but present. As a result, swimming in the Cheat is for the brave and daring. And there isn't much of it."

The watershed of the Cheat is more rural than that of the Monongahela. The latter is the larger river with a watershed made up of larger towns and cities. More drainage from construction and agriculture both streams into the Monongahela, and its water carries a genuine sediment load. The chief impairment of the Cheat, though, comes from acid mine drainage. There are more tributaries running with acid mine residue into the Cheat than into the Monongahela, but partly because the Cheat is used for fishing and boating, remediations efforts are underway. In 1994, a mine blowout galvanized reclamation efforts on the Cheat. An operator in the process of closing down the T & T Mine had decided to circumvent established procedures; because the company would be expected to treat the continuing acid discharge from the mine indefinitely, he chose, instead, to bore holes from the mine to an adjacent abandoned mine, assuming that the water discharged from his mine would converge with that of the older mine, lessening his treatment costs. Instead, the rerouted water ruptured the entire side of a hill in a blowout. In this case, bore holes were discovered, and there was no question as to who was at fault. Criminal proceedings ensued, as did the formation of Friends of the Cheat, a watchdog group committed to the restoration of the river.

Later that afternoon, Dennis and Marcia took me to Georgia's Creek, a tributary of the Monongahela, so I could see for myself the effects of acid mine residue on a river. Vestiges of the steel and coal industries were visible everywhere as we drove north along the river. A century ago, at the height of the steel industry, the steelworkers at the mills along the river called it "the river of sweat," and above Point Marion, the banks of the river are the site of industrial archaeology, both sides ornamented or littered, depending on how you look at it, with the remnants of their industrial past. Monolithic concrete pylons for barge tie-ups punctuate the landscape. Elsewhere, one finds the rusted steel pylons, the old, worn relics of sand and gravel pits, emerging from the surface of the water after so many years with a kind of perverse tenacity; the industries that constructed them may be long gone, but they reflect a decayed aristocracy, continuing to lean and teeter over the surface of the water, a generation of crippled descendants with their own dissipated elegance. An old conveyer line used to load railcars from trucks or barges hovers toward the river expectantly. So antique are these battered artifacts, so worn and weathered by their exposure to time and to the river, that they invite a certain sympathy; it is easier to view them as sculptural by-products of river life than as industrial intruders on the ecosystem of the river. I couldn't help but think of them as a kind of river architecture; the abstract language of form conveys a social history of the river narrated in a terse alphabet. Dennis, though, had little patience with this view or with them, seeing them instead as visual pollution and further proof that the river is treated as a junkyard.

The industrial residue in the creek itself was less elegant. Pyrite, a mineral that is exposed during coal mining, is full of iron, aluminum, and other trace materials, and when it comes into contact with water, oxygen, and bacteria, it becomes highly acidic. Acid mine drainage is a result of this leaching into rivers and streams, making them inhospitable to any kind of aquatic life. The rocks at the edge of Georgia's Creek have been stained a sickly, synthetic orange hue, and the water is stagnant. Remedial action isn't necessarily expensive; it requires grinding limestone, a neutralizing agent, into a powder and mixing it into the water, and water discharged from mines can be drained into limestone leach beds or guided through limestone channels which neutralize acidity. But this is a continuous process that needs to be done often and at the source of the drainage.

While effective, such measures are reactive. A more thorough and effective process would be to clean up the source of contamination at the mines themselves, but there is scant funding for such reclamation. In 1977, the Abandoned Mine Land Fund, a federal fund raised by per-ton tax on coal mined, was established to finance the treatment of continuing discharges from abandoned mines; but because these funds are also applied to other cleanup efforts—closing dangerous mine openings and removing highwalls, for example—many waterways continue to be impaired. The increase of AML spending would not only benefit the rate of reclamation and watershed restoration but also stimulate the economy of those West Virginia and Pennsylvania regions that have been plagued only by the legacy of coal mining.

While one might think that the Clean Water Act would have mandated remedial efforts for the river pollution caused by mining, the EPA, which monitors the execution of the act, has generally been lax in enforcing standards. The department established standards for amounts of pollutants that can be discharged into streams and rivers, and a protocol for monitoring those discharges, but both of these are observed irregularly in West Virginia, where the Monongahela and Cheat rivers originate. After the Clean Water Act was passed into law, guidelines were constructed sector by sector across the entire economy to determine how different industries could develop individual guidelines for compliance. The guidelines for the coal industry, established in 1982, are long outdated. Unlike what happens in many other industries, the way coal impairs a waterway has to do with rainfall: In dry weather, a mining operation might discharge little into a stream or river, but after a rain, discharges are increased. Guidelines for the coal industry are based on a series of rainfall exemptions, and such exemptions have routinely given the coal industry a pass on compliance. Not only that; there were far fewer effective watchdog organizations twenty years ago, allowing the industry and government to pass industry-friendly regulations with less scrutiny.

If a weak permitting system has delayed recovery efforts on the rivers of West Virginia and Pennsylvania, the coal industry has left another legacy that is more subtle and pervasive, one found not in the currents of the river but in those of public perception and behavior. Dennis and Marcia took me to Nemacolin, a company town built in the early 1900s. Its more than four hundred residences had been built as a model community by the Buckeye Coal Company, and its main street reflected from the outset the social mandates of the coal company: Single-family homes owned by bosses and management were built on one side of the road, two-family homes for miners on the other. Still, all residences were equipped with the amenities of the time: furnaces, indoor plumbing, electricity, and separate underground sewage and storm sewer systems. Nemacolin was named for a Delaware Indian Chief, and the word translates to "He for whom something has been envisioned," a phrase that has a certain poignance a century later.

The community had been governed by the company until the late forties, when the houses in the town were put up for private sale. The parent steel company filed for bankruptcy in 1986, closed and sealed the mine, and today the hospital, school, and movie theater are gone. Many of the two-family houses have a patchwork appearance, one half sheathed in vinyl siding, the other in peeling clapboards. Shingles and faux stone make an appearance as well, a material expression of the disconnect in the town itself. The Monongahela River flows at the foot of the hill below town, yet it seems off limits. The afternoon we visited, the steel gates to the road leading to the river were open, but the road that had been paved with brick in 1921 to lead from the river to the company store was unused, overgrown with trees and bushes, and nearly impassable, and the community's connection to the river was all but severed. An abandoned old brick building, once part of the mining operation, was crumbling, but reuse was not part of the conversation. When we saw some trucks parked off to the side of a dirt road, we turned around and went back up the hill. There was no sense of overt hostility, but Dennis was wary of how strangers would be greeted.

Envisioned as a model community, Nemacolin has evolved into a model of something else, possibly a timeline of environmental abuse. On one edge of town is a waste coal pile, the height of a twenty-story building. Piles such as this continue to emit low levels of sulfer dioxide. On the other side of town is the Hatfield's Ferry Power Station. Along

with the Fort Martin Plant just south of Point Marion, it has been designated one of the dirtiest coal-fired plants in the country. The designation is determined by the plants' emissions of lung cancer–causing
arsenic and beryllium; nitrogen oxides, which produce smog and further irritate the lungs; and sulfur dioxides, which can aggravate both
lung disease and heart disease and further contributes to ozone deple-
tion. Its smokestacks emit mercury content as well, a toxin that can
cause neurological and brain damage. Controls are generally viewed as
too costly. "How does a company on its last legs financially come up
with the money for controls?" Dennis asked. Fines are an option, as are
variances, but compliance seems a last and unlikely resort.

As is so often the case in economically depressed areas around the
country, the local population tends to remain indifferent to the health
hazards surrounding them, and there has been a near seamless trans-
fer of loyalty from the coal industry to the power industry. It is Dennis's concern that the power plants along the river have stepped in to
assume the region's historical allegiance to the steel and coal industry.
Certainly they have assumed the long tradition in the region of industry abuse of the environment. "The coal mining industry didn't
take the proper steps ecologically or environmentally to take care of
the people in the community," he told me. "There is a blind loyalty to
the UMWA. And the power plants won't be union plants. But people
will have jobs." And jobs are immediate, while long-term health remains an abstract concern. Despite the fact that cancer rates in the
county are several times higher than elsewhere, health considerations
remain distant.

This is something Dennis knows firsthand. When a public hearing was held in Nemacolin about the construction of a new power
plant, it was held in the town's union hall, a choice of location that reflects the spirit of current affiliations. He had helped to organize an
information meeting a few nights before. ("You don't learn anything
at a public hearing.") Sixty or seventy people showed up, he recalled,
but they were generally all in favor of the plant. There were no ques-

tions about the adverse effects such a plant might have on the health of local residents. "Forget about getting broad-based public support," he said. "No one wants to consider a recession." And he called the area a "sacrifice zone for electricity, or, actually, jobs."

Dennis is precise in taking measure of the physical world. When I had first phoned him about the swim, it hadn't taken him long to e-mail me back with some vital statistics: "I put a thermometer in the main channel on the Mon River today at about 10:30 a.m, with the air temp around 70° F. I came up with a water temp of 62°F . . . I paced the width of the river (using the bridge), and I came up with 144 paces. That's with the water level as low as it goes, so it could be a bit wider at higher levels." Those measurements were accurate, and there is little reason to think that his calculations about the health hazards of a new plant are any less precise. Besides, I know that he lives and works with another equation in mind as well, which has to do with the weight of human conscience and what it takes to put it to rest. When I asked him how he manages the frustration that is likely to come with his kind of activism, he replied, "You just keep doing everything you can as long as you can. Then you can at least sleep at night."

A week after my visit to Point Marion, the Houze site held an auction for its buildings and equipment. Marcia is a skilled quiltmaker, and it is one of her dreams to have an expansive studio in one of the factory's old industrial buildings where light would stream in through windows that offer a wide view of the river below. It's the kind of vision that has been realized in countless adaptive reuse plans for industrial space around the country, but here it seemed like more of a stretch. The night I spent at their house, I slept under a quilt she had made for one of her sons. It was a radiant patchwork universe stitched with vibrant images of a green earth and blazing sun, bursts of nighttime stars, and underneath it I had had a night of deep and dreamless sleep. As the community struggles to remake itself, one can only hope that her vision of the natural world will find some expression that exceeds the dimensions of a single quilt; and find some way to bestow a comfort that goes beyond a single night's sleep. Still, I was not surprised when I learned later that there were no bids on the Houze property due to concerns about a concrete-encased tomb of waste glass containing arsenic and cadmium.

The town hosted another event that week besides the Houze auction, and the two occasions seemed to reflect the two qualities that bracket the spirit of the community. If the Houze closing and auction spoke for economic decline, the Albert Gallatin Regatta reflected community efforts toward recovery and the conviction that the river could be the agent for this recovery. The regatta is named for President Thomas Jefferson's secretary of the treasury, who had built a house, Friendship Hill, just north of town. In previous years, the regatta had been oriented toward the water with canoe and other boat races, but this year liability concerns had reoriented the festivities toward land, and one of the main events was a five-kilometer footrace. But the hope was that with the new launch, future regattas would return to the river, and reestablishing the canoe races was already under discussion.

In an effort to change public perceptions about the river, the Greater Morgantown Convention and Visitors Bureau organized a triathalon that included a 1.2-mile river swim the following month. "The Mon has always been an industrial river, and for years it was not in good shape," one of the organizers told me. "But in the last twenty years it has been cleaned up tremendously. It's not a pristine body of water by any means, but it is greatly improved, and while the combined sewage overflow might make choliform bacteria levels go up in high-water days, on low-water days, the water is fine." The lock and dam upstream were shut off for the duration of the swim, temporarily restricting the flow of the river so as to allow participants on the preestablished rectangular course to swim in water without any discernible current. Of the some five hundred swimmers in the river that day, no one complained about the water quality. And if restricting the river's current seemed misguided—part of the beauty of swimming in a river is in getting to know its current, its flow, its feel, and direction, and prescribing a narrow course in a stilled river seemed an opportunity missed, a way to coerce a living river into imitating a pool—that it promoted river swimming at all was no small feat. A spokesman for the Mon River Trails Conservancy went so far as to say the swim had done more to change public perception about the river than years of environmental activism.

Morgantown is not the economically depressed town that Point Marion is, and with any luck, the benefit of such efforts will flow from one community to the other, connecting them just as the river does. And the fact that it is a north-flowing river speaks to the rewards of the unexpected; possibly, the river that defies probability in the direction it takes will also beat the odds in its renewal. To early pioneers, the Monongahela River was known as "the river of dreams," but only a century later, it had become "the river of sweat." Today it is both of those things.

Driving here, I had imagined a river that would challenge the mandates of the physical world, but it was not the course of these rivers that felt unnatural or illogical. What *did* contest the sense of rightful order were the generations of industrial abuse. But that's the thing about the unexpected; it's never what you think it will be. While I was grateful to have the St. Christopher medal, I found my-self leaning more toward another notion of a spirit force. When asked what he meant by the name of God, Jung answered, "To this day, 'God' is the name by which I designate all things which cross my willful path violently and recklessly, all things which upset my sub-jective views, plans, and intentions, and change the course of my life for better or worse."

Nothing about these two rivers crossed my path violently or reck-lessly, and even their northerly flow felt ordered and assured. Yet they challenged all my expectations. I think about the way the level of the water can rise without your ever noticing. And then I think of all the other things that are said to flow like a river: tears, wine, words, poetry, literature, music, love, hate, streets, roads, light, glass, steel. It's a start to know that these are all things that can move in any given direction, every which way, from south to north and north to south, and east to west and west to east. And then back again.

The Mississippi River

MULTIPLICITY IS IN THE character of any river. When the Nile flooded, the ancient Egyptians were prone to think of its waters as the tears of Isis. For the ancient Greeks, the river Lethe brought forgetfulness. In Thailand, *mae nan* is the word for river, and it means "water mother." In its continuousness, its source of fertility, its nurturing and life-sustaining character, the river is often regarded as a female deity. In Indian myth, the river Ganga is a place of purification and cleansing. The image of the river can represent the beginning of all life, but when it is the river Styx, the river is one of death. The river is what carries you away from home and everything you love, and it is what takes you back again. The river is what allows you to imagine that there are things that can go on forever. The meaning of the river may be as continuous and inclusive as water itself; and in trying to determine what a river represents, I would suspect that for most of us, these various meanings are layered in our minds and in our memories; all of them ring true in one way or another at different points in our lives.

Certainly that multiplicity of meaning resonates for me. That the blissful pool reflecting the leaves of the tamarind tree in the garden in Bangkok might also have been an incubator for *Mycobacterium tuberculosis* is the least of it. It also contains one of my earliest childhood memories in which I was drowning. As I remember it, I was in that little cement pool, and it was impossible for me to get my head up out of the shallow water. The sensation I remember most clearly, apart from being unable to breathe, is one of being twisted around and around in the water. The difficulty in finding air came from the sense of being caught in a spiral of running water and not knowing in which direction air might be found. Like so many childhood memories, it is nothing but a fragment, a scrap of recollection that, for all its elusiveness, left a genuine imprint. And yet, when I think back, I don't really know. Was it in that pool where I was momentarily submerged? Neither my parents nor my siblings ever mentioned the mishap to me, so who knows when or where it might have actually occurred, if it did at all. The other explanation, of course, is that it is some fragmentary recall of being born. And I couldn't tell you now, so many years later, which it was, birth itself or a near drowning. It never mattered much.

If a river can reflect so many meanings, there must be just as many ways to take measure of it. There are rivers where it is enough to glance at the width, take in the quiet current, and know that getting across and back is nothing more than an idle summer swim. In other rivers, you may want to know when it last rained, what water releases have been made by dams upriver, or what the bacterial counts are. And if it is the Hudson you are talking about, information may be found in the brushstrokes and texture in the paintings of Sanford

Gifford, because those also graph some essential information about the reflective play of light and water that identify that river. But the Mississippi River, our grandest waterway, may require a different set of calculations. Beginning in Lake Itasca in northern Minnesota, it runs a 2,320-mile course to the Gulf of Mexico; its basin covers more than 1.245 million square miles. Satellite images underscore that it is a river that knows the strength of its identity: Even once it flows into the Gulf of Mexico, it's in no hurry to converge with the salt water. Its dark ribbon of blue remains visible as it streams into the straits of Florida, rounds the tip of that state, and travels up the coast to Georgia, where it finally acquiesces to be absorbed by the ocean.

That was why weeks earlier I had made a call to Joel Asunskis, an engineer at the Army Corps of Engineers in St. Louis, to find out what the conditions of the river would be in mid-July. There are two ways to measure the current of the river, he told me then. One is to calculate velocity, determined by the number of feet the water moves per second. The second is to calculate flow, which is determined by volume and time. To be more accurate, velocity times the cross-sectional area of water equals flow. There are more variants in flow: As the water level of a river rises and falls, the contours of the bed change, and so too does its flow and velocity. Flow, then, is a better measure for the river than velocity. Asunskis had confirmed then what I already knew, which is that the river is at its lowest during July and August. Still, he had said to me at the end of our conversation, "I'm not even going to hint that I think this is a good idea."

His genteel reproach was reiterated when Onni and I got to Cape Girardeau in southeast Missouri; it's a town that doesn't do much to invite you directly to the river. Broadway, one of its main arteries, leads down the gentle slope to the river, but it does so without any genuine intention or sense of ceremony, as though the way in which the road takes you to the river is more a factor of random geographic happenstance than part of any deliberate plan to deliver you to America's grandest waterway. On a late summer afternoon, people had

found better things to do than hang around on the streets. Cape Girardeau is a college town, but Southeast Missouri State University had
shut down for the summer, and the pool halls and bars were quiet.
Restaurants, cosmetic stores, and hair salons were all shuttered and,
along with the abandoned storefronts, suggested the lassitude was the
result of something more than the heat of a summer afternoon. TRAIN
A CHILD IN THE WAY HE SHOULD GO AND WHEN HE IS OLD HE WILL NOT
TURN FROM IT, reads a mural on the side of a church. I am so desper-
ate to find some sign of the Mississippi that I take it to be some
oblique reference to the river; maybe it can be read as an instruction
about spiritual assurance that somehow reflects the river, just out of
sight here, flowing confident and secure in its direction. Because
there is nothing else to suggest that we are approaching the most
magnificent of all American rivers. Even when we reached the foot
of Broadway, where it meets the Mississippi, it wasn't the river we
saw, but the wall.

In his book *Old Glory: A Voyage Down the Mississippi*, Jonathan
Raban describes Cape Girardeau as a hostile and marginalized outpost. The city had made itself impregnable, he writes: "A gray concrete battlement, twenty feet high, had been raised around it to protect
it from the river . . . Its wall announced that it considered the Mississippi a dangerous enemy. The brute ugliness of the thing had fear
and dislike written all over it. Here was a town that was having as little to do with its river as it could possibly manage." To be sure, Cape
Girardeau may have been a walled and gated city. Its floodwall *was*
an imposition; it was meant to be. About a hundred miles or so south
of where the Missouri flows into the Mississippi, the city had endured
decades of periodic devastation, its homes and businesses deluged and
wrecked by the river's cyclical flooding. The Army Corps of Engineers began construction of the floodwall in 1956, and by the time
the seventeen-foot-high, four-thousand-foot-long wall was completed nine years later, along with a series of earthen levees, pumping
stations, and drainage structures, it effectively severed the city from

the river. For decades after, Cape Girardeau was directed toward another interstate artery, Route 55, a few miles to the west, that runs from Chicago straight through to Memphis; reoriented toward the interstate in a series of strip malls and big-box stores, its relations with the river had become tenuous.

Forty years have passed since the wall was built, and twenty-five have passed since Raban came through town on his boat. Approaching the city by land rather than by water today offers a different view. What had happened to the wall during that time is what happens so often to the walls people build: They crack, break down, openings are chipped away at. Probably operating with a similar mixture of tenacity and intuitiveness that had prompted the city planners in Sunbury, Pennsylvania, to look for ways to punch through their floodwall with plazas, perhaps, or steps and an amphitheater, the residents of Cape Girardeau have also managed to erode their floodwall. Which is not to say that it has been worn down in any apparent physical way. The floodwall remains as a massive concrete fortress between town and river, and the high watermarks concisely notated on one of its gateposts attest to its work. But through some kind of evolving community concensus, Cape Girardeau has managed to redirect its attention to its waterfront, recognizing the value of both its innate historicism and hospitality. After the construction of the wall, the immediate waterfront had been surfaced with cobblestones and chunks of limestone too rough to walk on; now, a smooth embankment with concrete steps invites you to sit and watch the river. The old brick buildings have been renovated, and a hiking trail along the river is being planned.

But it is the floodwall itself that has drawn the most attention. As part of a continuing civic effort to reconnect the community with its river, the city's River Heritage Mural Association commissioned the painting of *Mississippi River Tales* in 2002, and today, a series of twenty-four arched panels along an eighteen-thousand-square-foot section of the wall facing the city narrates the history of the city. Beyond the wall is a slice of river, nothing more than a sliver, but that afternoon, that bit of river was the only thing moving; and where the gates opened onto the river, wall and riverscape collaborated in a panorama in which painted images of the river seemed to flow and merge with the view of the actual river coursing just behind them. After half a century, the wall has managed to connect the city and the river every bit as effectively as it separates them.

Certainly the wall was what had brought me to this section of the Mississippi. Choosing what rivers to swim in had been easy at first, determined by sheer proximity. I swam first in those rivers of the Northeast that I had some passing familiarity with, that I had walked or hiked along, crossed on bridges or been on in boats, and one seemed to lead naturally to the next. But in this case, the River Heritage Mural Association had commissioned Tom Melvin, a friend of mine from college, to paint these murals, and throughout the previous year, I had been hearing about their progress. He and his crew had finished painting the wall in fall 2004, and the dedication had been scheduled for the following July; that sense of urban reinvention, along with the celebratory mood around the dedication and the chance to see old friends, seemed a fit and auspicious way to approach swimming the Mississippi.

Tom has a view of the object world that is as respectful as it is discriminating. In college, he drove a small black Corvair that he had inherited from his aunt Violet. The car had a rack on its roof, and among his friends it was always a subject of idle curiosity what might be found tied to the roof rack: Christmas trees, bowling pins, duck decoys, faux palm trees, orange traffic cones, a plastic macaw. I may remember a flock of penguins once being there too, but it is possible that I imagined that. The roof of Tom's car was always a place inhabited by imaginary constructs, and who could blame me thirty years later for confusing what was actually up there with what might have been up there. In the intervening years, he has lived and worked in Chicago with his wife, Nancy, and his signs, murals, and architectural illusions have managed to slowly braid themselves into the urban fabric, where his respect for historical detail is consistently matched by his reverence for the imagined world.

While the wall that Tom painted in Cape Girardeau has none of the exquisite chaos of his car rack, it is a similar landscape of unexpected choices. As elsewhere in his work, visual poetics and historical realism seem to converge inexplicably. He knows what there is to know about the placement of the stack on a locomotive from the late nineteenth century, but he has chosen to use a picnic basket, a controversial choice it turns out, to suggest the hospitality of Cape Girardeau to the Cherokee during their forced exodus to Oklahoma. He has taken pains to memorialize the Carolina parakeet, a species now extinct, in the inaugural panel, but that is not to say he is above accommodating the more commonplace cliff swallows which build their mud nests under the bridge.

What is most important, I realize, looking at this wall for the first time that summer evening, is that the river remains visible in nearly every panel. It appears beyond the painted arches as a thread of blue in the background of a panel that depicts Lewis and Clark's visit in 1803, and it is in the foreground of a panel that represents the flood of 1927: Flappers stranded in a flooded car are waving their umbrellas and cigarette holders. In a panel that shows Jean Baptiste Girardot, who established the original trading post, the monsignor is playing a fiddle, the long reach of the shimmering silver river extending behind him. In these ways and others, the Mississippi flows in front of and behind and around and through the history of the city, allowing the wall itself to serve as a view to the river.

Certainly that impression was reinforced later on in the evening. In the dusk of the July night, the riverfront becomes Cape Girardeau's village square. Couples have brought their folding aluminum lawn chairs out to sit on the embankment on the side of the wall that fronts on the river, the kids are sitting on the steps eating ice cream cones, and the teenagers are slouching on steps closer to the river—all of which made for a scene of communality. It's the kind of public promenade you might expect to encounter more routinely in the plazas of Italy and Spain than in the American Midwest, and I could see, then, that this is not the city marginalized from the river that Raban had described, but rather, one that has found its way back to the river.

A section of the wall on the far end of the other side had been painted by another muralist in the late nineties, and the *Missouri Wall of Fame,* as it is called, depicts Mark Twain, Rush Limbaugh, Burt Bacharach, Joseph Pulitzer, Dale Carnegie, Laura Ingalls Wilder, Calamity Jane, and T. S. Eliot, as unlikely a congregation of people as one could imagine. Yet the gathering tonight seemed to be some kind of parallel spontaneous party. I wondered if it is possible that in its own perverse way, the wall has made the river accessible to the town, as though its very surface and height have managed to create a kind of waterfront salon, defining a public space along the river and inviting residents to come on over.

And so we did. That evening, the river reflected the full spectrum of pink, violet, lavender of the sky, and the entire landscape, veiled in a thin summer haze, was painted in pastels. Even the low line of trees on the opposite shore seem to be a kind of pale, muted olive, as though the heat of the day had filtered the intensity of color and softened it all at once. The surface of the river, combed by the gentlest of evening breezes, barely feathered, appeared placid until I looked more closely, which was when I realized that the sense of orderliness was pure deception. Fix your eyes on something on the water's surface, a stick, a branch, a curl of flotsam drifting on the current, and the speed and strength, the sheer force of the current at once became apparent. This was water with a different weight to it. I understood now why the Mississippi has been designated a masculine river. Most rivers are thought of as feminine, as having a fluid and nurturing character, but the Mississippi is understood to be the king of American rivers. The name itself is derived from the Ojibwa name for the river—Messipi—which translates as "Great River" or "Father of the Waters." Even when it is called Old Man River, the meaning has nothing to do with being tired or spent, and more to do with its authoritative, commanding persona.

That flow is a more accurate measure than velocity came back to me then. Their difference does not come naturally. I find it almost impossible to make such distinctions intuitively, yet it seems like one worth trying to understand, as though it encodes some essential way to measure different kinds of human experience. Now, as I watched a log float down the river, twisting and turning in the current, knocked this way and that by the water, then vanishing, I was seeing some evidence of that equation: Velocity is simply a measure of speed, while flow takes into account the full force of the river. In his film *Rivers and Tides*, the Scottish artist Andy Goldsworthy says that "the river is a river of stone, a river of animals, a river of water, a river of many things. A river is not dependent on water. We are talking about the flow." He is an artist talking about a small river in Scotland, and yet he is echoing the words of the engineer upriver in St. Louis: To know the flow of a river, you need some passing familiarity with all its variants. Onni and I looked at each other. Even the Hudson at slack tide has a peaceable nature. But this was something else.

Before I headed down to the dedication the next morning, I paid a call on Anita Meinz at the Cape Girardeau Convention and Visitors Bureau. When six months earlier Tom had recommended that I track her down, I had thought that he was referring her to me in her official capacity as a representative of the city's tourism interests, which is what she does now that she has retired. He had told me then that she knew everyone in town, and when I had called her, I learned that she had spent much of her working life as the assistant to the principal at the Franklin Elementary School in Cape Girardeau; or, as she put it, as the "secretary, nurse, and general flunkie for twenty-seven years." Over the intervening months I had discovered that knowing how her students have managed to apply their early education in their continuing adult lives was apparently part of her job description. She knows what a lot of them are up to, and they're the lucky ones. In my search for an escort boat and pilot, more than one man told me that Anita was "like a second mother to me." Modern educators are fond of talking about classrooms without walls, but she gives new expression to the idea. Tom had not gone to an elementary school administered by Anita Meinz, but he hadn't spent much time in Cape Girardeau before he had taken to bringing her fresh flowers most mornings on his way to work on the wall. And she had found a place in the convention center for Tom to store his painting supplies. This tends to be how things go with Anita.

Despite being impeccably attired in a pantsuit, silk blouse, scarf, and makeup, Anita is an octogenarian trickster, with all the attendant wisdom and expertise. Chuck Martin is the director of the bureau, but Anita is the first person you see at the reception desk, and she operates with a certain efficiency. Possibly because she spent most of her professional life with schoolkids, she knows that you sometimes have to fool people into doing things. When I had asked her that day on the telephone who I might find to escort us across the river, she paused only slightly before saying, "I know just the fella." Jody Geiser was another student in her extensive classroom. Now Anita put in a call to Jody to get him down to the convention center so that we could meet. "Get on down here, now," I heard her instructing the voice on his answering machine. "You want to meet Akiko. She's kinda cute." Then she got off the phone and fixed her gaze on me. "I don't think he's the kind of man who's ever going to get married," she said, eyeing me conspiratorily and a little sadly. She was serious. The relevance of this news to the particulars of my own life was of little interest.

If the town has conflicting feelings about the river, they were fully reflected later that morning at the dedication of the wall. State and local political and business figures seemed genuinely pleased and triumphant that the mural had been completed; in the planning stages for decades, its completion signaled the revitalization of the historic waterfront. Strolling among the crowd was a dark-haired man in leather breeches, then a pair of women in long ruffled skirts, holding parasols. Among the models Tom used to paint the figures on the wall, they had put their costumes back on for the ceremony. Appearing to have stepped off the wall and into the morning, they meant to lend credence to the notion that the wall had animated the spirit of Cape Girardeau. Yet that never really happened until Tom got up to speak. As he took the podium to thank the town and talk about his experience painting the wall, there appeared to be a black man behind him hurling a bucket of water at his head. In fact, Tom was standing in front of a section of the mural depicting a slave extinguishing a roof fire, ignited when a confederate cannonball was shot into a residence during the Civil War. This trick of perspective was another of those alignments between the real and painted world that Tom manages to foster so effortlessly in his work.

At the same time, though, word of our swim the following day had gotten out, and we were accosted from all sides by disbelief; nearly without exception, the idea of getting in the river was anathema. Despite the fact that every frame of the mural celebrates the history of Cape Girardeau and the Mississippi River, almost everyone we encountered had something discouraging to say about our swim. "Better you than me," the mayor said to us, and when we were introduced to the president of Southeast Missouri State University, he seemed incredulous. "You're not really going to get in there, are you?" The fire chief was glowering but said only tersely, "I'd like a call from you in the morning before you set out." I was grateful for the concern, even though we had taken precautions, had arranged for an escort boat, and were not engaged in some foolhardy enterprise meant to put our own or other lives at risk. In the end, the simplest thing to do was simply to agree to make the call in the morning.

Not that their skepticism didn't make sense. For generations the chemical plants in St. Louis washed their refuse into the river. The

city also poured its raw sewage into the river until 1968, and even today, outdated municipal sewage treatment plants up and down the
river emit overflow into the river after heavy rains. River debris also
includes railroad ties, branches, stumps, whole trees, planks, pilings,
and whatever else the river can wrest away from the ground during a
heavy rain. With a size and force not always fully recognizable on
the surface of the water, these are the unseen obstacles lethal to
prospective water-skiers, Jet Skiers, and anyone else who might assume the Mississippi is a recreational waterway. And then there are
the marks on the floodwall indicating high water; during the flood of
1993, the river rose nearly seventeen feet above flood stage, and the
mark on the wall is well above my head. Living alongside this river,
you can't help but have mixed feelings about it.

Nonetheless, since my first phone call to Anita, I had heard the
stories of a local doctor who made an annual cross-river swim in
Cape Girardeau, and at the dedication ceremony, his name was in-
voked time and again. Yet no one could quite remember when he did
it, or why, and while the specifics of his swims have been forgotten,
they have become absorbed into local river mythology. The archives
of the local paper, the *Southeast Missourian,* said more. An obstetri-
cian and gynecologist, Fred E. Rawlins had started the swim as a
teenager down the river in Thebes. As he told the paper in 1999,
"When you're seventeen, you don't think about the danger. The river
was here, and I just wondered if I could do it." That summer he did
it without a boat, with nothing but some spare change to pay his toll
to get back across the river. Except for an eight-year period from the
late forties to the mid-fifties when he was in medical school, he made
the annual swim, usually on his birthday, continuing until he was
well into his eighties. When it came time for his annual swim in 1993,
the waters were high from the flood, but he went in anyway. "He was
probably washed down all the way to Thebes, but he still made it," I
heard. I recited these particulars of his story to myself every time I
was regaled with further discouragement.

By the time I met Cape Girardeau's police chief later that morning, I expected more of the same. But Stephen Strong narrowed his eyes as he looked at me. Then he looked out across the river. "It can be done," he said, and his words conferred an almost mythic consent. Then a moment later: "Besides, it's not as bad as what my mother used to do. In the wintertime, she used to walk across the river." On the mural near where we were standing was an image of the river during the Big Freeze in the winter of 1918 and 1919. The river had been wider and slower then, a time before the dikes and levees had been built, and during especially cold winters, it would freeze. This panel of the mural offered a view of the river as a solid, with massive chunks of ice piling up on one another. Off to the left was an old Model T making the trip across the ice floes, which was surely more treacherous than anything Onni and I had in mind. Strong went on to say that his mother walked across the frozen river in the twenties, when she was a teenager. "The river froze up and the ice was there, and she thought it would be an adventure. She had a friend, and they would get into trouble together. Or maybe she did it to say she did it. Once she got halfway across, she got concerned about how thick the ice was. She heard noises, the way you would. She could hear the water underneath and the sound of the ice cracking, and she got a little afraid, but it was too late then to do anything about that, so she just kept going to the other side."

Strong understood the importance of identifying people and places correctly. Her name was Helen Tuck, he told me. Strong had some sense of the order of things, and I wondered if it was a legacy from this woman who had walked across a frozen river as a teenager; she must have known something about order and physical borders, or maybe she just understood that the landscape can impose its own imperatives; ferries didn't run in the winter, and there were no bridges over the river between St. Louis and Memphis. "She was afraid of water and didn't know how to swim," Strong told me. "Maybe she did it because it was there." I have teenagers at home whose abiding attraction to danger fills me with dread, and yet I find myself feeling a distant affinity to this teenage girl some eighty years ago, and her decision to walk across the icy river, to cross an unfamiliar distance, and to answer to the impulse to make some kind of definite passage from one place to another.

Right about then, I found Jody, our river guide, in the crowd. His face has the sternness that only the truly cherubic can have, and over the past few months, he had given our swim serious consideration. The first time I had spoken to him on the phone, he told me how he had learned how to water-ski on the river as a child. He doesn't much swim in the river, he told me, but still "it's pretty smooth. Besides, you know rivers. You float 'em more than you swim them." I knew then that I had found a confederate. He told me how he had worked for twelve years as an engineer on the railroad, making the run from Cape Girardeau to St. Louis, until an injury had forced him to quit the job. Now he worked in a family-owned business in real estate and property management, but he missed the river, and one of the things he missed most were the eagles. "You'd see hundreds on every trip," he said. "Bald eagles. You'd see the little ones, and the old ones too. Sometimes they would float right down in front of the engine, and you're doing fifty miles an hour or so, and then they would just veer off. That's what I miss." The Mississippi is a working river, and he knows that better than anyone; there isn't much recreational boating here. Still, he spent as much time as he could out on it, and he pulled out the map to show us the course he had charted.

Cape Girardeau was named for J. B. Girardot, who established a trading post near Cape Rock, a massive rock promontory that juts out from its west bank just above town. The river bends just above Cape Rock, and that bend, along with the thin tributary that flows into the east side of the river, makes for a current that is in a state of confusion and swirling with eddies. A quarter of a mile or so below Cape Rock is an ongoing dredging operation that keeps that area of the river clear for the towboats and barges. But below Cape Rock, the river narrows, and if we started our swim on the Missouri side between those two spots, we could aim for a sequence of thin sandy beaches on the Illinois side; if we missed one, no matter, we could just aim for the next one downstream. Jody had charted the river the way you might diagram a sentence—subject, object, preposition, verb—and he explained its syntax to us. "You've got more of a runway on the Illinois side," he told us. There are some pilings jutting out into the river more or less directly across from the marina, he pointed out, and we could come in just above those. The main thing was to reach the other side before the current swept us down to the highway bridge on the south side of town; the river is fast there and widens slightly, and forms eddies around the bridge abutments. "It would be good to stay away from that." Jody knew the river enough to be pragmatic about the swim. "It's low now," he said. "And there isn't much debris. You should be fine."

We decided to meet the next morning at the convention center down by the river. It wasn't until we got there that we saw the morning newspapers with their photographs and headlines of the train and bus bombings in London the day before. Some conspiracy of elements—maybe just that ordinary sense of remove that travel confers, the heat of the Missouri morning, and the wide river running just yards away—had put us at a distance, conferred that kind of disassociation that comes so effortlessly to all of us as citizens of the information age. And yet I thought back to that small photograph of us at the river almost four years earlier that was still tacked to Onni's wall and wondered at the universe of small recoveries that had already started a continent away.

Anita's desk seemed a fitting departure point, and we were not disappointed. She opened a drawer and offered us chocolates that had been given to her by Martin Strel, the marathon swimmer from Slovenia who had swum the entire length of the Mississippi in the summer of 2002 in an effort to promote peace, friendship, and clean water. When he got to Cape Girardeau, Anita told us, a summer storm had come up, with lightning hitting a buoy only feet away from the swimmer. He survived to send chocolates to Anita, she said, and around about then, I saw Jody rolling his eyes. "She was my principal's assistant," he said. "She ran the place just like she does here." But the fact that Strel's epic swim was commemorated by these chocolates seemed an auspicious send-off, as did the fact that we had picked up an unexpected participant. John Wyman, a local businessman, had heard about the swim and wanted to come along. As the owner of some of the restaurants in town, he might know something about the graciousness of setting a place for the unexpected guest, I thought, not to mention the luck it sometimes brings. After all the dire warnings we had gotten, the presence of a spontaneous accomplice, and a local one at that, seemed to confirm that swimming in the Mississippi was not so far-fetched an idea. I ate a chocolate. I picked up the phone and left a message for the fire chief. John's teenage daughter, Murielle, came to see us off. "This is fun," she said. "No, I mean this is crazy."

We didn't take much along. A towel. Sunscreen. Onni had a pair of goggles. That was about it. We both had water shoes, but these felt more like an assault on logic than anything else. They had been advertised as "sea to shore sports shoes" and even "sports shoes that swim like a fish." They are able to float, have mesh uppers and perforated orthotics that enable them to drain, and are apparently equipped with an emotional life as well: Their promotional material attests that they love the water. But no one needed them. It is said that you can tell much about a culture by the shoes its people wear, and the most these did was remind me of the excessive measures we take when we are unsure of how prepared we are. The water shoes, I knew, would be left in the boat.

Jody had arranged for us to go out in the river with Greg Sparkman, who ran a local boat dealership, and he was waiting for us out at the launch with a sixteen-foot Glastron that was so new it didn't have a name yet. The two of them are self-styled riverkeepers, and I don't know whether it is in spite of this or on account of this, but all of a sudden, both men became pranksters. People who have some kind of essential information or whose field of interest has some innate gravitas often need to leaven that with humor. They reminded me of a surgeon I know who will do stand-up comedy at a moment's notice and whose taste for two-headed nickels and whoopee cushions has accompanied him through his adult life, as though the significance of his chosen work has somehow necessitated the creation of a comedic alter ego.

"You're gonna have to watch out for those Asian carp," Jody warned us. "Don't be surprised if one of them jumps up right next to you." He went on to spin an outlandish tale about how these gigantic fish had been known to leap into boats and onto barges, flopping around on the deck, startling their captains, and causing all manners of navigational chaos. The possibility of such cartoon characters entering the frame of our swim interjected a levity into the morning that had been absent in the litany of harsh warnings, and even the shepherd's hook that Jody had brought along "just in case one of you needs to be fished out of the river" was straight out of some vaudeville routine. Moments later, Greg and Jody were both scrupulously outlining a complex rescue maneuver apparently favored by Native Americans that involved fully submersing the swimmer. I saw now that they were the slapstick docents of the Mississippi because they couldn't help themselves, howling at their own hilarity. Then Greg told us with a straight face that the most valid way to judge the distance across water is the Native American way: You bend over and look at the water from between your legs. Right. And then suddenly, despite the months of anticipation and planning, our expedition, with its jokester pilot, unexpected guest, and nameless boat, was infused with ambiguity.

Up by Cape Rock, the water was roiling in huge swirling eddies that looked to be miniwhirlpools. They appeared suddenly at this bend in the river, and just as quickly, the river took on a different persona, one of unexpected turmoil. The dangers we had heard so much of on the Susquehanna had been subtle, invisible, but this stretch of the Mississippi didn't hide anything and put its trouble right there on the surface for anyone to see. This was feral water that boiled up and circled in and around on itself, then cascaded back in on itself again. Downstream were a couple of parked barges and a crane, all part of a dredging operation, part of the continuous effort to keep this section of the channel clear, and somehow the generic hum of its engines rang true, as though it was some kind of soundtrack for these vortices of swirling water. I imagined the rushing boils of water circling in on themselves in some parallel manufacturing enterprise that was generated by an independent force and energy of the river's own. Cogs in the river's labor and industry, these pools passed themselves off as pieces of fluid machinery on the river's vast and complex assembly line, indifferent to anything that came in their way. I read these coils of water as the signature of the river's contempt. Nothing would get me in the river here.

But then Greg swung the boat south again, and just as quickly, the water calmed. Despite the fact that John was scanning the surface of the river for signs of venomous cottonmouths, the quiet surface of the river brought a wash of relief. There are surely those people whose inner mathematics tell them that if there are whirlpools upstream, there will be whirlpools midstream and downstream as well. That could be true, but my own calculations are based on a conviction that the earth is a place of balance and measure. To me, if the river is turbulent upstream, downstream is where it will be subdued. Like anything else in turmoil, a river looks for chastening. So it was with a sense of relief that I realized Greg had cut the engine and was drifting in slowly to the shore. When he suggested we jump in, I was happy to do it.

The river's clear persona from the evening before had vanished, and in its place was a density, an opacity. It carried mud from the Missouri downstream, picked up its own load of silt and sand, and it had carried the tugs and barges and every other manner of watercraft imaginable, and it is nothing to the river that three swimmers have been added to its freight that morning. As best as I could tell, the river was about a half mile wide here, and for the first twenty feet or so, where the water was calm and the current negligible, its force still remained palpable. Then, suddenly, we were caught up in it. Midriver, there were no immediate landmarks, and it wasn't until I looked back to the shore where we had started that I realized how quickly we had been swept downstream. The fact of the matter was that the water didn't seem to be moving so much, but the distant shoreline was breezing by at a steady clip, a perception that says something about our inability to assess our whereabouts when circumstances around us are changing fast. Jody had warned us that the current would hit us quickly and unpredictably, but still, it came as a surprise. And there was no point in doing anything but swimming downstream with it.

Then, just as quickly, the current was again quiet. We were in the middle of the Mississippi River, which I was astonished to find was a gentle stretch of water. It offered no resistance; swim a few strokes in any direction you chose, and that's where you'd go. Swimming against a strong current, your body intuitively calculates what it will have to do to meet the force of the water, but here the resistant stream had been dissolved. Adaptability is so often viewed as how we rise to meet some sort of adversity, but how we adapt to the unexpected gift of ease and comfort is no less important. Onni floated by alongside me and said, "Boy, that doctor sure knew something that no one else knew," and I imagined him on his solitary swims year after year, decade upon decade, and wondered if he had ever gotten the rhythm of the thing; if he had ever learned to anticipate the uncertainties of this current, if the language on this stretch of water had any constancy, or if he had been surprised as we were every time he did it. He was always accompanied by someone in a boat, I had heard. And he had told the newspaper, "You have to have someone to point the way, unless you swim early or late in the day. You can lose your direction unless you're watching the sun." He had said this after he had been swimming across the river for sixty-five years. My guess is that the language of the river, like any other, has its own variances in grammar, its own changing rhythms.

I thought of a complaint voiced from time to time that summer by one of my sons, a novitiate poker player. "I was just left on the river," Noel would say at the dinner table, with all the anguish and resignation that comes so naturally to teenage boys. People find a way to learn what they need to know, and the year they were sixteen didn't seem to me like a bad time for my boys to learn about the coalition between luck and rational choice and about how the occasional coincidence of pure good fortune and intelligence can be one of life's great gifts. Where better can one be left than to drift and float with the flow of the current, I had thought then. But it signaled a more dire circumstance to Noel. Being left on the river, I came to learn, had something to do with being left with the last unlucky card in the last hand of the game. The game of poker came into being on the riverboats of the Mississippi, so there was a logic to the way his words revisited me. Now I would know how to answer him; being left on the river may not be so much about being displaced or adrift as about trying to comprehend the language of the water, learning to anticipate how the current threads the river, and knowing where the creases in the surface of the water reflect a change in its force and direction.

Because then, again, without warning, the river seized up in another rush of current and washed us downstream again. I had been told that the river was low this time of year and quiet. The drought had lowered the level of the river, and just a few weeks later I would read about how the river traffic had been stopped entirely because the water level was too low. But none of this came to me then; the river felt fast and strong and unpredictable, and I gave in to it. I found that if I didn't fight the current and just submitted to its draw, I had little sense of its speed or volume or flow.

As we continued to be swept downriver, our destination kept changing. First it was a bit of sandy beach on the opposite shore, then a bank of mud, and later, a low stand of willows farther downstream still. The river's shipping channel is marked by a series of green buoys on the west side, red buoys to the east, and the red buoy I was sure I had been swimming toward was far upstream by the time I reached the east side of the river. Not that it mattered. The failings of observing the linear route are familiar to me. This route across the river wasn't any more direct than the river itself, and there was no good reason not to change our destination in what became a diagonal transit downstream, though certainly not a direct diagonal, but one that looped in and around and back on itself before continuing. It confirmed my preference for the indirect approach and verified what I already knew, which was that there are times when a straight line is impractical and ineffective; and that there are places—and people and things—that cannot be arrived at directly. Coming at an angle to things, even if they are nothing more than some scrappy sandbar willows, accommodates all the shades of motive and desire, all the vagaries of human inclination and intent.

On this particular morning, that route was also a luxury. If some conspiracy of natural forces, intention, and human limitation usually dictate route and destination, this morning we could go anywhere we might end up. I looked back to the west side of the river and could see that we had washed down almost to where we had started at the boat launch across the river. Tom and Nancy had come to the boat launch to see us off, and I could see them now sitting on the rocks, Tom in his red hat, and Nancy in a white summer dress, channel markers of a different order in a vignette of repose that could have been taken from a panel of the wall he had painted. But by then the water was moving so fast again that I needed to look straight ahead. And I wondered if this was something I'd have occasion to do again, just change where I happened to be going based on how I was getting there.

The current stayed just that strong until we were within a few feet of the eastern bank. Nothing much was there, just some swampy woods and a riverbed that's a wedge of slick, slippery sludge; between that and the current it was almost impossible to get a foothold, and every time I thought I'd found my bearings, I slipped. For all the discouragement we'd heard before we set foot in this river, the Mississippi didn't make it any easier to get out. Finally, though, at the bank where the water was only a couple of feet deep, I managed, and suddenly I was there, standing up. A few thin willow saplings and a knot of dry bushes were at the water's edge, which happened to be a strip of mud, parched and sun-cracked. "And I didn't see a single cottonmouth," I said to John, and without missing a beat, he answered, "No, but this is just where you might see one sunning on the bank over there." I looked back up the river to the place where we had started, and saw that it was maybe half a mile away. If I hadn't been able to look back up the river, I couldn't have said whether we'd been washed downriver a tenth of a mile or two miles. That was what the current was like, just some mystery you're in the middle of until you're out of it.

Experience is not always easily distilled into words. Martin Strel's last words in his written account of his sixty-six-day swim were: "Frontiers are in one's head. The limits of capabilities, limits of fear and courage, borders of a country. We break them and set them. We live and we die. We spit and greet." I knew that the stilted language had to do with how the words had been translated. Still, a kind of logic attended the awkward syntax and vocabulary of Strel's narrative, and trying to maintain my balance on that slippery mud bank, it occurred to me that I could use a translator myself. Sometimes a particular experience requires its own language, possibly even its own obscure and spontaneous pidgin, and at that particular moment, standing in the mud on the edge of the river, "we spit and greet" sounded about right.

After Greg picked us up, he took us for a cruise downstream under the bridge. Moments earlier, the Mississippi had been a difficult river to get out of; now it was hard to get off of it for a different reason: There seemed to be some unspoken consensus to stay out just a little longer. Murielle was laughing at her dad, but he was already thinking about doing it again, next year, and maybe the year after that, like the doctor, an annual swim. "There was nothing to it," John said to himself, out loud. When we finally got out, I tried to offer Greg some form of payment—for his time, for the gas it took to take the boat out. But he wouldn't take a dime. "I had a pretty bad week," he told me. One of his employees had quit, and he made a vague reference to other troubles closer to home that had been plaguing him as well. He didn't elaborate but just said, "Coming out here is what I do to get rid of the stress."

Later that night, we walked back down to the river. Tom and Nancy showed up with a few of their friends from Cape Girardeau, some of whom had helped paint the mural, others who had helped out as models. Anita was there too. It was Tom's last night in town, and we all had a few drinks, and it only seemed right to take in the wall one last time. We joined the group and strolled from panel to panel, but it was folly. The illumination from a few streetlights wasn't all that great, and somehow trying to make out the images in the mural in the darkness of the summer night made me feel a little more drunk than I was. Not that it mattered. I realized that if a group of people who have had a few drinks are all doing their best to decipher these images in the dark, the wall has more than done its job.

I took in Broadway one more time before we left in the morning. I knew coming here that this was America's grandest river, but I had had no real *sense* of it. I thought back to what had brought us here, what logical progression of events and places had gotten us to the Mississippi, and whether I could possibly believe that the Hudson River, the Delaware, the Connecticut, and the others that followed had collaborated in their courses to bring us here. Of course they hadn't, any more than this hot empty street with a shuttered hair

salon, a couple of pool halls, and some darkened restaurants are a logical avenue to the Mississippi River. One minute you're staring into
the window of an empty coffeehouse or running your hand across
the dusty window of a tired pool hall, and then the next thing you
know, you're face-to-face with the wide, ceaseless, green current of
the strongest river in the country. But that's probably just the natural
rhythm of things. Life doesn't often tell you when it's going to offer
you the momentous thing, the person or the experience that comes to
matter most. You don't see it coming, and half the time you don't
know it even when it's happening. If you're lucky, though, you might
pick it off later; looking back, you might say to yourself, "Yes, that
was Big." I met my husband when I was in college, waitressing, and
the afternoon I slid a beer across the table to the guy in the blue shirt,
it never crossed my mind that I would spend the better part of my life
with him. And the morning my mother was unable to pick her comb
up off the shelf, she assumed it was a muscle spasm in her right arm
rather than a malignant brain tumor.

I picked up a cup of coffee down by the river and drove out to Cape
Rock for a last look. The roiling whirlpools of water below were not
in my line of vision, and nothing in the view from the outlook spoke
to the imminent sense of peril you feel when you are on that stretch of
water. A few minutes later, a beat-up, old white Plymouth cruised up
the road and parked, and I recognized the man who climbed out as
being one of the regulars down at the waterfront. He started up the
path to the lookout and was looking at me as though he knew me,
which made me nervous as it was still early morning and we were the
only ones out at this remote spot. But the minute he started to speak,
it was clear that it was just the river he wanted to talk about. He'd
seen me taking notes and sensed that I could use some more information about this river. Gary Scheper is a rural mail carrier, but he
told me that he preferred to think of himself as a riverwatcher. "On
my days off I try to find how many places you can see the river from
Sainte Genevieve to Dyersburg. I've probably missed some of them,"

he admitted, but I got the feeling he hadn't missed many. He told me he'd found twenty-five or thirty spots where you could get a good view of the river, some from overlooks like this, other ones just offering a good sight line through the trees. He'd got pictures of pretty much all of them. "Down in Columbus State Park in Kentucky, they got part of an old chain that the Confederate soldiers strung across the river to keep the union boats from going downstream," he told me. "You oughta go over there. I think they've still got a few old links of the chain." I asked him how he liked the wall. "Yes and no," he told me. "Mural improved the looks of it, though."

The morning was shining. I looked down at the Mississippi. It had a pink and golden glisten from the morning sun glancing off it; there was not a barge in sight, and the river seemed momentarily at rest, far removed from the muddy wash of alternating currents I had been immersed in a day earlier. A hundred and fifty years ago, Mark Twain wrote *Life on the Mississippi*, and in a section of the book called "Further Complexities," he admitted, "Two things seemed pretty apparent to me. One was that in order to be a pilot a man had to learn more than any one man ought to be allowed to know; and the other was that he must learn it all over again in a different way every twenty-four hours." It occurred to me that may be another way of saying that the variants of flow are infinite.

And I thought of all the views to the Mississippi that Scheper had found, and of all the panels on the wall that Tom and his crew had painted, and I realized that this was the way it is with this river. The scenery changes. It requires that many views. Its rhythm is the rhythm of change. In his *Mississippi River Journals*, John James Audubon documented his travels by recording each bird he observed. On this stretch of river: "I took a walk to a Sand Barr where Joseph Killed a Large bleu Crane, unfortunately a Young one—saw few Geese, many Cardinals. Some Carolina Wrens—We are better today—Luckily our boat does not leak—Saw a few Purple Finches." Bird by bird, he had learned the river. But the view of the river could just as well be the perspective of a fearless teenage girl in midwinter, or all those views that an eighty-year-old doctor acquired across a lifetime of annual swims, or the conviction of a Slovenian marathon swimmer promoting goodwill. You can love a river and never want to get in it. A wall can unite as well as it divides, and you can hate it as much as you love it. Yes and no. None of these things are ever as fixed as we would like to imagine. Maybe that's another way to take measure of a river—in pieces, frame by frame, panel by panel, view by view. Maybe later, they'll converge into a single stream where I can take in the full measure of its flow.

The Ohio River

T HE ROAD THAT TOOK us out of Cape Girardeau seemed a route to infinite sufficiency. Once we'd crossed the Mississippi into Illinois, Route 3 took us north, parallel to the river, and on either side the landscape leveled off into the flatlands of the American starch belt, its vast acres of emerald rice paddies and fields of corn and soybeans stretching as far as the eye could see. I could think of few other places on this earth where such excess is so orderly, so neatly and capably managed, regulated into such precise rows and grids. The few farm complexes we passed bore no resemblance to the rambling old barns of New England that are familiar to me. Because I was raised in the Northeast, my idea of a farm involves some sort of familial enterprise; farming begins in a sense of intimacy, with pastures tucked in between hills or scrabbled together after wood-lands have been cut, some kind of exercise in faith and persistence. In the last thirty years, multitudes of these family farms have closed up shop, and I saw now what they have given way to.

These farms in this valley were on a different order of magnitude, sprawling agro-industrial complexes, with gleaming assemblages of silos, loading ramps, conveyer belts, and massive equipment sheds. Acre after acre of leveled fields practically vibrated with a kind of mechanical repetition, an agricultural assembly line that suggested that the rhythm and pattern of farming have been as flattened as the land itself. It was easy to lose sight of the fact that any of this is about the cultivation of organic matter or that the wide river is just to the west, its water table beneath us seeping up into the fields.

It produced a kind of vertigo. It wasn't just the visual confusion that is, oddly enough, the result of excessive regularity in the land-scape. The eye begs to swerve, to bend the line of vision, to find some distraction, to search out irregularity, because it knows that too many straight lines that go on for too long cause some kind of disbelief that human labor can extend itself in such straight lines, a monotony that seems lacking in humanity. Or at least that is what I thought until we stopped at a crossroad farm stand in Ware to buy tomatos, peaches, blackberries, melons, and the shopkeeper behind the counter, in a gesture of kindness that somehow tempered all the rigid geometry of the fields around us, did his best to persuade us to take some of the produce that was going to be past its prime in a day or so. "Here, take it," he said. "It's more than we can use."

But no sooner had we headed east, away from the river and into the Illinois farmland, than the landscape became more arid. That it had been a dry summer became increasingly apparent as we drove across the toe of the state, heading toward Golconda, on the eastern border of the state where the Ohio River divides Illinois from Ken-tucky. It didn't end up being much of a destination. By the time we got there, Golconda had shut down. It was a Saturday morning, and the farmer's market had just closed, the streets were empty, and the town had that sense of vacancy that is more familiar to me in winter when a hard snow keeps everyone indoors; here it was the other extreme of weather that was keeping people in, or so it seemed until we reached the parking lot at the edge of the river.

Our first real glimpse of the Ohio was across a gleaming acreage of cars, pickup trucks, and boat trailers, their metallic surfaces rippling with reflections of light and water, a hard-edged river of its own. The parking lot stretched to the river, a contemporary equivalent to the Hadley Green. The Ohio itself was thick with fishing boats. Although the river is wide here with a broad ramp leading to it, the access is for boats, not swimmers, and a thick morning haze seemed to flatten the river, making it distant and impenetrable. Maybe it was Jody's maps, his deliberate planning, and the route he had carefully charted for us on the Mississippi, but that morning, determined as we were to find a place to swim the Ohio River, we had done nothing more than just point the car east to see where it took us. I could scarcely stand to open another map or guidebook, and had relinquished for the day any idea I might have had of being an informed traveler, but looking across this wide green streaming river with no place to swim, I began to question the strategy.

We drove to a state park outside of town in the hopes of finding some other way to get to the water. Where the trees dropped off, we could sense the nearness of the river, but we couldn't see it, or hear it either, and certainly there was no way to get to it. The only other human we saw was a man sitting still in his white Toyota in the parking lot. When he saw that we were examining a map, he came over to see if he could be of any help. "I just come up here and wait," he told us. "I'm waiting for the deer. I like to take their photographs," and the lazy nature of his lingering already seemed in synch with the spirit of the day. He gestured to a thicket partway down the path where the arrival of his subjects was apparently imminent. When we asked him where we might find access to the river, he shook his head. Finally, when pressed, he suggested we head up to Bell Springs, an hour or so to the north. It's not on the river, but it's still a place to cool off and swim, and at that moment, it seemed like destination enough.

Bell Springs. The name practically vibrates with clarity: The ring of the man-made object and the geologic phenomenon are both characterized by their sense of clarity, and the two words, when coupled, suggest clarity taken to an extreme. But when we got to Bell Springs, we found the granite canyon and its confluence of streams bone-dry. The dusty corridor of the rock walls seemed to be little more than a construction meant to absorb and radiate pure heat, and the streambeds themselves were parched gravel scars. I stepped over the carcass of a desiccated frog. Like people, the natural landscape is capable of having a shadow persona, and that morning Bell Springs seemed a deception of a name, a word, a hope. It was barely midday, but the futility of reaching water in this dehydrated landscape was dawning on us. I knew that it was my own fault for acting on such whim, for relinquishing a plan, for choosing chance and serendipity over forethought. On our way out of Bell Springs we passed a small graveyard, which, inexplicably, was outfitted with a mailbox, its little red flag raised. I couldn't imagine any reason for it to be there, and yet, on a day when all of our own endeavors seemed to be marked by equal measures of persistence and futility, it had its own perverse logic and it became a reasonable icon for the day.

And so we did then what people sometimes do when there is a stretch of road and when they have no particular purpose or direction or are simply discouraged, bored, or tired. We just drove, and then drove more, south and then west, until we ended up in Metropolis, Illinois. Situated on the Ohio River just downstream from where it converges with the Tennessee River and just upstream from where it meets the Mississippi, the city is a small but precise index of American fantasy. It was founded in 1839 as a hub of river transportation, and when the railway displaced those dreams and possibilities, Superman came along. In 1972, the town officially declared itself the hometown of the man of steel. (That Clark Kent came, in fact, from Smallville and went to work in the fictional city of Metropolis was of little matter.) But even Superman couldn't shoulder the burden of urban decay on the river town; when the oil embargo of the mid-seventies slowed the influx of tourists and the completion of the interstate was delayed, plans for the construction of the two-hundred-foot-tall Man of Steel were replaced by a seven-foot fiberglass statue. Today, the largely abandoned and boarded-up main street has the all too familiar feel of an American river town down on its luck.

The glittering apparition of purple glass and pillars of faux marble at the end of the city's main street where it meets the river appeared, then, as some mirage produced by the heat and stupor of the summer afternoon. This was meant to be a riverboat, I knew, but the lavish incongruity of its sparkling entrance façade against the quiet backdrop of the Ohio River positioned it in some more generic landscape, possibly that bleak intersection where the brazen appetite of commerce meets unrelenting human expectation. Maybe it only made sense that on a day our luck hadn't held out at all, we came upon Harrah's riverboat, a four-story extravaganza squatting at the river's edge. The casino arrived in Metropolis in 1993. "Harrah's Metropolis brings the pulse-pounding Las Vegas atmosphere straight to you," says the casino Web site, which I visited later in trying to figure out why it's here at all, because traditions of riverboat gambling notwithstanding, Vegas seems a curious way for a midwestern river town to reclaim its identity. If the hope was that gaming revenue would reverse the community's decline, I saw little evidence that any such thing had happened. Despite the casino's gaudy promise that "there's a slot machine for everyone," the quiet of the town had less to do with a sleepy summer afternoon when it's too hot to be out, and more with a continuing economic slump.

Even the Super Museum at the other end of town seemed desultory on that summer afternoon. Posters, mannequins, fabricated cutouts, and an inflatable Man of Steel perched near a window all outnumbered the people on the street, suggesting this was not a museum so much as the superhero's spawning ground, and predictably enough, the very profusion of figures served only to diminish his stature. A couple of tourists were posing to have their pictures taken with the statue erected outside in Superman Square, but the fact was that in this age of supersizing, the dimensions of the mannequin at the tire franchise on the strip outside of town exceeded those of the superhero.

The state park at Fort Massac just outside of town has river access, and down at the waterfront a coast guard cruiser was coming in. I figured that's where we might find some information about where to swim the river, but the officer I spoke to was circumspect. "Do it at your own risk," he told us, "but you probably ought to have a boat. There's a lot of traffic on this river." He paused, then added, "Actually, the reason we're out here this afternoon is that we're looking for a body." A boat had capsized earlier in the day, and a passenger was unaccounted for. And finally he sighed and looked out over the water and said, "I wish I could just jump in with you." Instead, though, he waved us upriver a few hundred yards to a sandy beach right below a bend in the river.

A barge had been parked in the small inlet at the bend, keeping this part of the river well out of the flow, and though the water looked to be quiet, stagnant even, we decided to go in anyway. There was no chance of a cross-river swim here—the river is far too wide and the barge traffic too steady to consider swimming very far into it without an escort—but by that hour of the afternoon, all we wanted was to be in the water. And what I found once there is that the river might as well have been a lake or pond, because there was no trace of current to animate the water. The river here felt as listless as it looked, and as I happened to feel, every bit as sluggish as the towboats parked with their silent, hulking barges up and down the river, waiting to make the trip down the next thirty-five miles or so to the Mississippi. Even the silt on the riverbed had nowhere to go, and once we stirred it up, small clouds of muddy water hung suspended beneath the surface, adding to the day's catalog of lethargy.

Still, this spiritless little swim was a good exercise; this patch of turbid water articulated everything that was missing: the fluency, the sense of time and passage and destination, the feeling of being caught up in a flow that is coming from somewhere and going somewhere else. And I realized then that if cognitive maps are a way of organizing the environment, some of the rivers in mine, from time to time, are sure to be dull and sluggish. We seemed to have come upon some small, joyless stretch of the Ohio River that had no urgency to get anywhere. Anything you do that fails to live up to expectation and desire can clarify just what you are looking for; in this case that happened to be a sense of being consumed by something new and fast and different and outside of myself. Part of what I am after, I realized, is newness, strangeness, the untried, and the unknown. Not that I don't recognize or value the comforts of the deeply familiar. The repetition of domestic life that is so stifling to some is balm to me, and I have structured my very life around it: the kitchen table that asks to be set, the clothes that need to be folded, the porch that needs to be swept. Making a small corner of order for me and my family is what I have staked my life on, and I know and count on the solace that is found in the rhythm of tucking the boots under the bench and hanging the coat on its hook. But if I find reassurance in these gestures, it is because all the while I know that the natural world holds out both a grander chaos and a grander order, and that all the rivers that run through it stream with the vibrance and energy of the unknown. All of which is why this tepid little patch of stilled river did nothing for me.

Afterward, we stopped at the visitors' center at the park to change into dry clothes, and outside, we found a gathering of men in breeches and women in antique cotton dresses. They were weaving baskets and caning chairs. As it turned out, they were reenacting the activities of an eighteenth-century French settlement that once stood on the spot. "We usually do something with a more military theme," one of the women said to me, "but today we thought we'd try handcrafts." At that particular moment, both of these enterprises seemed equally incomprehensible and irrelevant. It seemed a small vignette of absurdity, and in our day of getting nowhere, just another exercise in pointlessness. Maybe it was the faux domesticity that rubbed me all wrong; if finding a stretch of river to swim in is some effort to escape my domestic order, this little farce of household handiwork grated on my nerves. Fort Massac is the very place where Meriwether Lewis had stopped in 1803 to find additional volunteers to take with him on his expedition westward up the Missouri. He had been disappointed in the quality of the men he had found in the garrison there, I had read, and I took a small, vicious pleasure in imagining what he would have made of their descendants, these faux settlers inexplicably caning their chairs two centuries later.

That evening we drove across the Ohio River to Paducah, Kentucky, where we found a different kind of historicism at play. The historic downtown district had been cleaned up and renovated, and was the backdrop for the town's ongoing summer festival. There was a display of candy-colored vintage cars, and street bands had set up, with the choices ranging from country and western to gospel to some teenagers who were going for heavy metal as best they could. Residents had set up their plastic lawnchairs to listen, and a few couples were dancing. The riverfront itself was alive with people eating ice cream and playing with their kids and lingering in the summer evening; what they were doing most of all, though, was watching the river. There had been a bass fishing tournament, and some of the contestants were going over the day's events. "I was out there today, but I'm just a candy-ass fisherman," I heard one of them say, and the tone of his self-assessment seemed to fit with the lazy atmosphere of the evening.

When we finally found a restaurant, it came as no surprise that two of the waiters had just quit. The sole remaining member of the kitchen staff who had been pressed into service as a waiter seemed more amused than inconvenienced by the flow of exasperated diners, and his charmed acceptance of the evening's decline was worth noting. Assuming that we needed to be placated, he brought us each a glass of wine, then another, assuring us these were on the house. Somewhere in my mind it registered that this was important, and that there are rewards to be had for getting nowhere, and if those rewards tonight were to be wine on the house, that's the way it was going to be. Midway through the second glass of wine, I began to feel as though learning to honor inertia would be an easy thing to do. That night at the campground, the low drone of barges on the river and the humming of the cicadas formed a scrim of summer sounds, a persistent soundtrack to my dreams.

The next morning, we noticed our neighbor at our section of the campground. He was sitting by his campfire, boiling his coffee, gazing into the middle distance. The intensity of his solitude was apparent even from a distance, and it made us nervous; we had the innate misgivings women sometimes have about men sitting by themselves, staring for too long at nothing in particular. Yet when I spotted the contents of his pickup in the parking lot, it was easy to excuse him. Hanging against the window in the cab was a row of neatly ironed shirts, and somehow these did something to civilize him. He was on his way to a family reunion, I thought, or to be the best man at his brother's wedding, and he had the look of someone who was soaking in all the solitude he could get. The handiwork found in these shirts with their artfully pressed collars and cuffs was infinitely more resonant than the faux caning exercise down by the river; this was domestic work at its best, infused with quiet purpose and order, evidence of the assured and deliberate attention on *someone's* part. Someone had cared enough about him to iron his shirts, or he had cared enough himself, and those shirts hanging against the window smoothed out the creases in my distrust.

At the Paducah waterfront, a sense of quiet theater persisted. Maybe it was the broad concrete steps of the embankment, but the invitation to sit and watch was compelling. Two teenage girls were wading, deep in conversation, and from time to time one of them quietly splashed the other; a fisherman ablaze with tattoos unhitched his boat from his pickup and slowly set off on the river for catfish. A man wearing a straw hat had a Weimaraner on a long leash and was encouraging him to dive into the water from a ramp that led to an abandoned barge. The dog crouched, peered into the water, leaned into it with his full weight, then dove in. My friend Brooke once told me she had an ancestor who painted the small animals in the paintings of John Turner. Turner was a master of incandescent clouds, great billowing skyscapes, the entire opera of the sky, but it seems he couldn't manage a howling dog or a frightened rabbit. Or maybe, too preoccupied by the transcendent, he just couldn't document the ordinary; at least he *knew* that the sublime needs a little of the prosaic at its edges. This morning, these routine events at the water's edge underscored the full spectacle of the river just beyond.

The very word *Ohio* is Iroquois for "Beautiful River," and the French called this body of water "La belle rivière." Pale green and threaded with silver, the river was well over a mile wide here, and pleasure boats, fishing boats, and barges drifted by. Midriver, I knew, the current was fast and strong, but here, lapping gently at my feet, the river felt almost gracious. I walked down to the water's edge, and it had a clarity and a sweetness. It was cool to the touch, but not too much so. This was easy water.

The idea that there is a slot machine for everyone revisited me, and I couldn't help but think these people out on the river on a Sunday morning were already having better luck than their compatriots in the casino just a few miles downriver. None of these events were of much interest in themselves, yet there was something mesmerizing in the way their improvisational choreography unfolded. As someone who once lived in New York City, I am familiar with street theater of all kinds, but what appeared to be river theater made for a lyrical and idyllic alternative.

These are people who love their river. For the last twenty-five or thirty years, Paducah has sponsored its own cross-river summer swim open to anyone who can complete the twenty-lap qualifying swim. The swim isn't competitive, and it's not a fund-raiser; it's just part of the town's ongoing summer festival and is about the pleasure of swimming across the river. Nowhere on the river are there warnings not to get in; nor is any stigma attached to swimming in the river. Nor is swimming in the river limited to this annual ritual. "See how clean and pretty that water is," said one of the fishermen, and when we told him we were hoping to take a swim, he said, "I'd swim in it too, but I can't now. Too fat. Some people say I'd float, but I don't even think I'd do that very well." He laughed.

Another told us of his own swim across the river one morning when he just got it into his head to go across the river. "Current's strong," he said. "It took me all the way down there," and he pointed to a grove of trees about a quarter mile down the opposite bank; yet it seemed to me a quarter-mile displacement on a swim that covered over a mile wasn't too bad. But then he added that he was fishing now. If we were around when he got back, maybe he'd have time to spot us. Hitched up to eight barges, a towboat, the *Marquette Transportation,* was changing its crew, and when I asked, the supervisor of the shift laughed at the idea of spotting us in his small skiff. "Don't have time," he said, "and the company wouldn't think much of it anyway. Liability concerns." One of the fishermen we had spoken to the night before swung by in his truck. He leaned out of his window to chat with us, and I saw on the dashboard a collection of sunglasses, at least ten or twelve pairs, with their assorted lenses of cobalt, midnight, deep sepia fracturing the light streaming through the windshield. It filled me with hope, this collection of lenses; any man in possession of such a collection must pretty much know what there is to know about enjoying the outdoors. But then he said, "I'd take you girls out today myself, but my boat's in another county. And besides, I still can't decide between spending the day at the river or the lake."

I looked across the wide river again. "It looked so beautiful, as though it were just waiting for us that morning," Onni said to me later. What had begun three years earlier as just something to do on a summer morning had become in the interim a mission. In going from the Hudson to the Delaware to the Connecticut to the Susquehanna, we seem to have acquired a sense of urgency. It began as a simple desire to cross a single divide; everything else was extra. But at some point all those extra things began to accumulate, and in the same way that counting laps eventually gives way to a less quantifiable distance, they began to add up to much more than we had anticipated three years earlier.

Perhaps, too, that urgency was articulated by the sense that this river was slipping away. A morning haze had settled in, putting the distant shore at an even farther remove. The Ohio at Paducah was the single river running through the single town where we had found a population who cherished the river, loved being near it, on it, and in it. We heard nothing about hostile currents, of contaminants, of leaks from the barges, of excessive mud and silt; from no quarter came the advice we had heard so often concerning our apparent need for medical intervention, be it a tetanus shot or psychiatric evaluation. And still, it was slipping by us, this river that we were not going to swim across, and it was clear to me then that I had miscalculated. Our trip to the Mississippi had mandated advance planning: coordinating with Tom and Nancy and the dedication of the wall, scheming with Anita as to which of her former pupils might make a reliable river guide, the rendezvous with Jody, and then his own strategizing that had led him to find Greg and the boat with no name. Our days in Cape Girardeau had been a result of precise planning, forethought, and deliberation. But anyone who has ever been on a road trip anywhere knows that it is easy to have too much of these, so almost as a contrary impulse, then, Onni and I had both left this trip to the Ohio up to serendipity; we were counting on happenstance, and even worse, luck, and we should have known better, because counting on luck usually tends to diminish any possibility of it showing up. The three people we had asked to spot us across the river all had better things to do, and I was reluctant to keep on asking, certain now that the river spotter we were looking for was, and would continue to be, otherwise engaged.

I wondered whether it was possible to think that I had already swum this river. I swam across the Monongahela River on May 21. That was fifty-one days ago. It's probably about 70 miles from Point Marion to Pittsburgh, where the Monongahela joins the Allegheny River to form the Ohio, and another 950 miles or so from Pittsburgh to Paducah. But this was a different river and different water; even if the current was running at three miles an hour, the water I swam in May was more than two thousand miles downstream by then. It was impossible, of course, for my numbers to accommodate all the fluctuations of current or to account for the variables in river flow and velocity, and I recognized this to be the worthless arithmetic of imagined accomplishments, the useless calculations of missed opportunities. As much as I tried to find ways to absorb the experience of swimming across this river by reevaluating and reinventing another earlier swim, it didn't add up. The truth was that we had missed the Paducah cross-river swim by two weeks and that the spotter I had hoped to find at the Paducah marina was elsewhere engaged. Later in the summer, I would learn that low river levels due to a drought had forced all barge traffic on the river to be immobilized; that, too, would have made our swim easier to manage. And I thought, then, of all those things I had failed to do because the time wasn't right, because I was off by a minute or an hour or a day, or if the time was right, because there was an insufficiency of courage or a dearth of conviction.

We were stalled in this landscape of dreams deferred. Our intent of swimming across that river was just as evanescent as those plans of the day-trippers at Harrah's or the kids at the Super Museum or the actors weaving their baskets at the faux French settlement. What seemed to me the spectacular failure in crossing this river generated an inflated sense of the unfinished, and my disappointment bloomed into an exaggerated sense of loss; concealed in the vast, wide surface of this river were all the things I never did but should have, all the things I should have said but didn't, the lost opportunities, the unspoken words, all the times my boat was in another county and all the times I couldn't decide myself whether to spend my time at the river or the lake. In college I had once imagined getting a degree in art history and learning everything there was to know about Piero Della Francesca and his use of the color blue. When I was in my twenties I understood little about making a home for my young stepson. And I know now the words of reassurance I might have said to my father before he died, but they did not come to me when I was thirty-one. And that knowledge was all there in the river along with the apologies I owed and the gratitudes I should have spoken, admissions I might have made. All of it was sweeping by me in that strong silver current; no wonder this river of the undone suddenly seemed so deep and wide.

In the geography of rivers, a meander scar is a riverbed that has been abandoned. It is the channel left dry when the river has rerouted itself or been diverted or when water has been drained from the channel for one reason or another. Channels can shift over time, their course migrating, and a meander scar is the vestige of that migration. It is evidence of the flow that once was there. But it is also a phrase that has a certain allure, because it says something about both the changeable nature of flowing water and the trace it leaves when it is gone. It is the vestigial river. The wide green Ohio River, running its long, deep course and assured of its direction on this July morning, was about as far from a meander scar as you could get, but still that was how it would linger in my mind, following that contrary path that memory so often takes when it insists that we remember the people and places we love not for what they are but for what they are *not*. It was not the Ohio River that had been diverted or changed course, but the ease with which my own will and resolve could be so quickly deflected. "Nature is our widest home," the writer Edward Hoagland said, and I saw then how such a home holds out the possibilities not only of endless excursions and discovery, but of uncertainty and stagnation as well.

We drove down the river to Cairo, Illinois, and later that afternoon while we were sipping iced tea in the luncheonette, the woman sitting in the booth across the aisle advised us to go to Fort Defiance to see the confluence of the Mississippi and Ohio rivers. "One's clean, and the other's dirty," she told us. "You can see them both." When we stopped there later and climbed the steps of the concrete observatory, I could see that she was right. The Mississippi had not seemed to me to be a river of mud the day we swam across it, but it began to look that way now, with the clearer green waters of the Ohio flowing alongside it. A mother was there with her two young boys, and the little one, maybe he was six or seven, was heaving stones into the river with great urgency, trying to mark that line where the two currents and two colors converged. In advising painters on how to best represent water, John Ruskin suggested studying its surface disruptions. "The only thing you need to be told is to watch carefully the lines of disturbance on the surface, as when a bird swims across it, or a fish rises, or the current plays round a stone, reed, or other obstacle. Take the greatest pains to get the *curves* of these lines true; the whole value of your careful drawing of the reflections may be lost by your admitting a single false curve of ripple from a wild duck's breast."

It is sound advice, I know, to try to ascertain the essential facts about anything, or anyone, by noting its response to disruption, and this boy throwing rocks into the river had instincts that were exactly right. His talent for distance and exactitude may have been limited, but no one cared. He knew that something was happening here, and he wanted to mark the spot. Onni and I both have two sons, and though ours are older than these two boys, we watched this woman reflexively, as one does a compatriot. Her boy's small arm didn't have the strength or muscle yet to throw the rocks very far, but he just kept throwing them anyway. She was observing him and at the same time settling into the stillness of her own experience in some exercise of watchfulness and patience that was familiar. I was reminded of everything I love about being a mother.

And then I was aware, suddenly, of a breeze, and the rustling in the leaves of the linden trees and willows. "It's the only place in the three-state area where the air is moving at all," said Onni. The water was moving fast too, and the sullen, summer day suddenly acquired its own energy and momentum, and I realized then that it was also the energy and electricity of all the things I had done meeting up with everything that might once have been possible, but that I never got around to doing.

The Current River

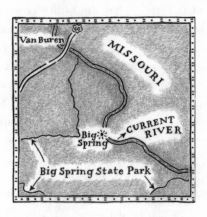

O N MY DESK RESTS a cobalt blue glass inkwell that had belonged to my grandmother. Its faceted sides form an octagon,
and it is decorated with an enamel floral design—a butterfly, a branch,
some pink and white flowers on gold branches. I have never put the
inkwell to its intended use, but its presence nevertheless performs its
own small function. There is something about the way the light
passes through the cut glass and sometimes casts small prisms of blue
light on the wall or window that speaks to the mystery of how experience and ideas can be distilled into words. Looking into the pool at
Blue Spring, I thought of that inkwell, and imagined myself to be
peering into its interior.

Blue Spring is very, very blue. It is that kind of Windex blue that is always astonishing when encountered in the natural world. Certainly it is astonishing situated in the more subtle gray greens and soft browns and ochres of the wooded hills of the southeastern Missouri Ozarks. The Osage Indians called it the "spring of the summer sky," but to me it looked more like a small piece of St. Thomas had been airlifted to the American Midwest, because it has a kind of tropical flashiness; it would look synthetic if you thought there was any way it could be. And it has the brilliance and clarity of the inkwell. Instead of a butterfly and blossoms, it is framed by different mosses, ferns, watercress. A red cedar bends over its bank. White stones lie at its bed. I imagined that bed to be twenty, possibly thirty feet below the water's surface because I could see it so clearly. In fact, the spring is 310 feet deep. As the park ranger told us, if you immersed the Statue of Liberty in Blue Spring, she would be immersed with five feet of water over her. "Her torch would probably go out," he added.

When I asked him what caused the intensity of color, his first answer was "because God wanted it to be," which is not a wholly unsatisfactory answer: The clarity of the water is such that it is at once a place of utter mystery and utter lucidity, surely a benchmark of many spiritual matters. But he eventually came around to telling us that the color is, in fact, due to the dolomite, a kind of limestone, that the water is filtered through. It is also said that the spring's blueness is derived from mineral particles in the water that disperse the reflection of light in a way that intensifies the color. RANKED AS THE 8TH LARGEST MISSOURI SPRING, IT IS CONCEDED TO HAVE THE DEEPEST BLUE OF ALL, reads the sign at the spring posted by the Missouri Conservation Department, and this genteel language hints at disputes about its hue that were solved in a gentlemanly way. That there are such arguments at all makes sense, because these bluest of blue springs proliferate in this part of Missouri. All of them are formed by water that becomes acidic as it seeps through the earth and eventually erodes the porous dolomite bedrock. The rock then forms cracks, and when the water finally breaks through these cracks, the springs are formed.

Alley Spring, about twenty miles east, has a similar placid surface and hue to that of Blue Spring, but because it does not have quite the depth, the argument could be made that its color is without Blue Spring's intensity. At Big Spring, the water surges out from the base of a dolomite cliff much closer to the surface, and the spring is a cascading torrent of blue foam with a daily flow of about 276 million gallons. Blue Spring has a daily flow of 90 million gallons. The deep underwater cave in the funnel-shaped basin of Alley Spring issues a daily flow of 81 million gallons. The subterranean rivers that beget these springs follow a different course than that of rivers that run visibly over the surface of the earth. Underground rivers are more dimensional; such rivers run, truly, more like the blood in our veins in that they can flow down hills, around them, and up them too, wherever the water pressure is strong enough to push them. The temperature of all these springs is consistent, because the temperature of both cave air and spring water is determined by the mean annual temperature. Whether it is January or July, the water and air remain between fifty-six and fifty-nine degrees. The streams into which the spring water flows are crystal clear. Beds of emerald green watercress on pale gravel beds give them a dappled appearance, like a pinto pony, Onni said, and that analogy captured both the patches of vibrant color and the fluid movement of the water. And where the water of all these springs eventually flows to is the Current River. In the same way that a small Victorian inkwell can represent the beginning of a sentence or a story, these blue, blue springs of southeastern Missouri are where the Current River begins.

Hearsay and nothing more had gotten us to the Current River. Maybe it was something about the silt and the mud and whirling eddies, the driving current and the sheer strength of the Mississippi, something about its endless procession of barges and towboats, but anytime we asked anyone in Cape Girardeau about the Current River, the tone of their voice changed, became more quiet, as though this was a river that occupied a different landscape not only in the state of Missouri but in the human imagination. This was a river, I came to learn, of clarity and stillness. "It's the clearest river you'll ever see," Jody had told us, and he told us, too, that over 70 percent of the river's water came from deep natural springs hidden underground and that it ran this clearly along its full course to the Black River in Arkansas. He told us about the hunting cabin he had there and how he would drive down on weekends when he could to spend some idle time on the river. If the Mississippi is a working river, the Current River, only some hundred miles away, is a place of quiet refuge. When Jody talked about it, you almost felt as though these two very separate rivers ran down either side of his life, a set of fluid brackets that marked most everything he did.

What Jody said had been repeated often in Cape Girardeau. "It's the prettiest place in the state of Missouri," we heard time and again, and "It's the clearest river you're ever going to see." At the Convention and Visitors Bureau, no sooner had we asked about the river than Chuck Martin had grabbed a map off a shelf and highlighted our route there with a yellow marker. His thick yellow line ended at the town of Van Buren, just north of where Big Spring pours into the Current River, and the circle he drew there seemed to brighten up the whole lower quadrant of the state like a little yellow sun. So maybe it was Jody's tone of voice, or Chuck Martin's yellow line; maybe it was the inertia of our day trailing the Ohio River; or maybe it was just the promise of a beautiful river, a clean river, a river hospitable to swimmers that was so alluring after our Mississippi swim. Looking back on it, though, I think what drew us most to the Current River was the idea of seeing how it was possible for something that begins in such genuine mystery to end with such absolute clarity.

We had left Cairo in early afternoon, taking Route 60 across the vast industrial grid of corn and soybean fields that make up the farmlands of southeast Missouri. In such flatlands, the dramatic scenery is often encountered in the sky with its cascading cloudscapes and rolling shifts of color, but in the oppressive heat of the day, even the sky was a white plane, a flat surface that seemed only to reflect the heat of the day back at us. It wasn't until late afternoon, when the yellow line delivered us to the foothills of the Missouri Ozarks with its forests of white oak and sycamore, that we found any kind of relief. By the time we got to Van Buren and turned south to Big Spring where it pours into the Current River, that air had cooled more.

You may find people who will tell you the Current River is for canoeing or for kayaking. Or tubing or fishing. Or for river excursions on the flat-bottomed johnboats that are traditional to this part of the country. But about 75 percent of the river's water is supplied by hundreds of natural springs, of which Big Spring is by far the largest, and that is what it makes it, most of all, a river for swimming. To begin with, this clear, deep, cool river water comes from a supply that is inexhaustible. We'd been driving most of the day, and by the time we got to the campground at Big Spring, we needed to find a place to buy some food and a place to pitch the tent. But the bright yellow circle on the map drew us first to the spring. The technical description for Big Spring is that it is a first-magnitude spring, which means that it churns out more than forty-five thousand gallons per minute. But neither numbers nor any rate of flow are what the eye registers first or what the brain first supposes when it encounters this torrent of blue water. My first impression was that there was more than enough. Far more than enough for us all. And any glimpse of such sufficiency in the natural world, for a moment anyway, quiets the soul. Yet for all its magnitude and excess, the spring itself is also a fragile ecosystem; because of its consistently cool temperature, plant life is often that indigenous to colder climates, possibly even a vestige of glacial movement, and the appearance of unfamiliar mosses and algae contributes to the sense of mystery. Even the slightest intervention can disrupt the delicate balance of aquatic life; there is no wading, much less swimming.

But a quarter mile away from the confluence of the spring's branch and river we found a campsite, and not far off, a sandy path that led to the river. The path wound through a scrabbly woodland of oak and sycamore, but then, just before it reached the river, a stand of giant cane. Though native to the region, the cane had nearly disappeared entirely after being used for generations to feed livestock, and its appearance now seemed almost exotic. But that is a common game that the natural world often entertains us with when it toys with our perceptions and expectations, presenting us with the native as exotic, and the alien as indigenous. Where I live in the Hudson Valley, thickets of purple loosestrife amass in meadows and wetlands by midsummer. The spiky, magenta spears of color look to be an indigenous summer bloom, and it is hard not to admire the way this lurid botanical infantry carves its way through the dense foliage that can seem so suffocating by late August. Yet they are interlopers, having only arrived from Europe in the early 1800s. Seventy-five years ago, the plant became aggressive, and today it chokes the marshes and wetlands of the Northeast, displacing the cattails and compromising and reducing the breeding habitats of wetland species. Still, after so many years, it seems of the place. And along the tidal marshes of the Hudson, tall stands of phragmites have insinuated themselves. With their flat, tapered leaves and spiky flowers, they appear as native, although they, too, are late arrivals that threaten to choke the wetlands. Yet here, by the Current River, the slender stalks of bamboo that towered and bent over us conveyed an inevitable Asian elegance that seemed curiously out of place in the Ozarks, as though the woods were somehow setting us up for the serene elegance of the river itself. And while all of these, the canebreaks and the loosestrife and the stands of phragmites bloom with confusion, toying with our ability to decipher what is native and what is not, their deceptions are, in fact, part of the protocol of the natural world.

Suddenly we were there, at the quiet ribbon of sparklingly clear, deep, cool water. Above us, on the opposite side, were sheer limestone cliffs, and gravel bars emerged in the river downstream, but we found ourselves standing at a sparse yet hospitable gravel beach along the water's edge. Although not far from the spring, the water here felt warmer, near the high seventies, cool, but hardly frigid. Which explained why, even though it was late afternoon by then, I was anxious to be in the river.

With its unceasing supply of water, Big Spring may give that section of the Current River a sense of sufficiency, but the character of the river is defined by the springs in another way too, which has to do with its proximity to the unknown. The pool at Big Spring has dimensions that can be seen, verified, measured. At the same time, because the source is out of sight, hidden deep within the ground, it alludes to a subterranean circuitry of chambers and caves, a vast interior network of waterways that are destined to remain unexplored; their depth, narrowness, and low ceilings all make them inaccessible to divers. It is also a network that is constantly changing. The rainfall that seeps into these systems becomes highly acidic as it passes through the layers of decomposing leaves on the forest floor. As it reaches the porous dolomite, it is perpetually carving out new chambers and circuits. The entire region is what is known as a *karst landscape,* a reference to the kind of earth that is characterized by its porous underground rock which yields a landscape of caves, springs, sinkholes, and immeasurable underground lakes and streams. The caves and caverns of Big Spring, then, have never been fully identified not only because the sheer amount of water and its force have never allowed divers to investigate its interior, but also because their identity is never fixed. Lack of established knowledge has led people to do what they always do when they don't or can't know something. They guess. Possibly the water comes from sources as far as the Great Lakes or Montana even. But who can say?

It is in the nature of the Current River to allude to the indefinite, and I found a small joy in that as I stood by the water's edge. So much of what I do as a writer and as a parent has to do with understanding why things are as they are. Why was this building sited this way? Why does the page look the way it does? Why did you say that? And why did you stay up until two in the morning when you had an exam the following day? Why didn't you tell me how you felt? It is by necessity that I, along with most of us, expend time and energy on learning how things have come to be. Or not. Information is knowledge, I tell my sons. Learn whatever you can. Gather the facts. Find the reasons behind things, and then you will understand them. This is all important and true, I know, and yet Einstein said that the "most beautiful thing we can experience is the mysterious. It is the source of all true art and science." To find myself now at the edge of a river with unfathomable origins brought a certain thrill. I am happy to be reminded of the realm of the inexplicable.

When I stepped in, the water had a coolness, and its texture was soft, almost silky. (I still find it odd that all water has a texture.) Although it deepens quickly, this is not a muddy, silty riverbed that pulls you in, but one that is clear about where the water stops and the ground begins. The bed of the Current is composed largely of chert, or flint, a sedimentary, quartz-based rock that is characterized by its hardness. The same material from which Indian arrowheads are made, flint is harder than glass and traps dirt, helping to retain the river's absolute clarity. The rocks and even the huge rootwads from fallen trees submerged in the water like some kind of clumsy infrastructure all declare themselves; even the filaments of light streaming through the water appear as some subaquatic circuitry installed to illuminate the river. This is a river that radiates with visibility. I think back to the Connecticut River and the abyss concealed in its black silt and to the Hudson and its landscape of hidden shipwrecks hundreds of feet underwater, and I remember how those invisible worlds are essential to the character of those rivers. I wonder whether the very lucidity of the water of the Current is some kind of gift that is meant to compensate for the enigmas of its source and origin. I know, of course, this cannot be so. Nature's gifts come without such compensations, and it is only my own mind that is trying to apply some logic and order.

I have begun to think that those of us who derive comfort from rivers do so because, in one way or another, all rivers are about carving out space. They are about ice and water and the force these gather in trying to find their way. Some do it voraciously and with aggression; other do it with a simpler persistence. It can take seconds or centuries, but all rivers are about making a place for themselves. We are after the same thing, trying as well to find some place on this earth that makes us feel as though we belong there, some crevice or path or course, some sense of give in the earth and rock that will allow us to pass through. The Current River seems to have made a place for itself with ease. I don't know if this is true or not. A year earlier, swimming in the Hudson River at Newburgh, I had been aware of the cut in the mountains just downstream, and of how the path of the river was the violent act of a glacier thrusting its way through rock millennia earlier. But the hills of the Ozarks were formed not by such a glacial flow or by the collision of tectonic plates, but by the more persistent erosion of rock by water. It is likely that the Current River carved its course with some degree of upheaval and disturbance; but from all appearances, it still looks to have arrived at a peaceable treaty with the rock around it.

Swimming across this river is a matter of swimming up it and down it and becoming familiar with its pull. The river isn't much more than fifty yards across, but still, it can take you any which way. The current is not so strong that you can't swim up it, but still strong enough to make floating down it a pleasure, and because it allows such drift, it is also capacious. It is an irony of swimming in rivers, and probably one that translates to other things as well, that a wide river with a strong current offers you fewer choices—it demands a plan that is expedient and efficient, a transit that is linear and direct. But a lesser river like this has more leeway and room, and though it is not a wide river, it has a spaciousness of its own. So I floated on my back and looked up at the sky and was reminded of my friend Emily, who teaches swimming to children. Four years earlier, when we had swum across the Hudson that first time, she had laughed at the absurdity of it. "Floating, it's just ludicrous," she had said. "It's one of those things you do successfully by doing nothing. You just lie there perfectly still. You give in to total stillness. It's about faith and trust. And I just get incredibly happy when I can teach someone to float." It makes sense to me that excursions on the Current River are called *float trips,* a term new to me, but certainly one that seems to have all the self-contradiction of a journey that is based pretty much on doing nothing.

The artists Christo and Jeanne-Claude, famous for their oversize environmental installations, are in the process of researching a proposal to stretch translucent fabric in eight separate sections down a forty-five-mile stretch of the Arkansas River in Colorado. *Over the River*, as the installation is known, proposes that 962 panels of fabric be attached to steel supports to create a textile wave shimmering eight to twenty-five feet above the water, mirroring the river and repositioning it, flowing, continuously, overhead. The Bureau of Land Management is considering the environmental impact of such an installation and evaluating objections that range from increased human traffic to the dangers the canopy would hold for low-flying birds, among them bald eagles, that feed along the river to the possible disruptions in the feeding and watering patterns of the bighorn sheep that graze along the river. But I remember thinking, as I float on the Current River and imagine such a wave of fabric stretched out above me, that the greatest sin is the excess of human desire, greed even, to imagine a river not only underneath but suspended overhead. The river as a vast, reflective ceiling is almost too much to ask for.

So we floated and then we swam about a couple of hundred feet upstream to another thin gravel bar. These beaches up and down the river are the unintentional legacy of the vast logging industry that reconfigured the Ozarks in the decades after the Civil War. As the

forests of native yellow pine were cut and milled for postwar building, the topsoil of the hills, with little to keep it in place, washed into
the river, often reshaping it and creating thin beaches. But in keeping
with its hospitality, or so it seems anyway, the Current River found a
way to accommodate this intrusion a century ago, turning it to its
own advantage and creating a series of beaches that intermittently
frame the river along its entire course. Now, generations later, these
beaches, a pale pinkish brown flecked with gray, emerge softly, sometimes at midstream, sometimes at water's edge, and appear to be part
of the river's natural topography, providing those who use it with a
place to picnic or camp.

Unlike other bodies of water, it is in the character of a river to con-
vey the passage of time. A still pond follows no clock, and in its endless cycle of tides, an ocean has simply its grand, rhythmic repetition.
But velocity and time are natural colleagues, and because it moves and
drifts and runs with its own current, a river follows its own clock.
And the time the Current River takes is gentle and manageable; even
its name is a reflection of that. The river was named by early French
settlers who called it "La rivière courant," or the running river, but
the name also has an innate redundancy; a river is a current and a
current is a river, and its meaning flows effortlessly back into itself.
Other definitions of the word *current* go farther in capturing the nuances of the river's name. "Passing in time or belonging to the time
actually passing," reads one definition, and others refer to "course, as
of time or events," to "the rate of flow," to "prevalent," to "publicly
reported or known." And while all of these meanings seem to converge naturally in this river, a different and more relevant way to
understand time and the Current River is to know this: If you are
paddling a canoe, you can go about five miles an hour down this
river; if you're just drifting in a tube, it's likely to be two or three.
The measurements for indolence on a summer afternoon lie somewhere amid these calculations.

"The only reason for time is so that everything doesn't happen at once," Einstein said. While this statement came from one of the finest minds of modern times, it seems to me it is also a sentiment that could be voiced by anyone who has spent much time on a river, because a river, almost any river, is that feature in the natural world that embodies almost everything there is to know about patience and impulsiveness, and the rhythm these can establish. Floating on the Current River, I became certain that how we think of time, whether we innately believe that time is short or that we have all the time in the world, is every bit as important, probably more so, than whether we are Type A or Type B personalities, how we think about sex or money, or whether we tend to be cheerful or depressive, outgoing or shy. How we perceive and use and experience time passing is vital to the way we experience life at large. I am certain that we are born with a view of how time passes. My son Luc gulps it down in huge breaths, then is just as capable of stretching it out interminably; he is extreme and excessive in the way he understands and uses time. He has all the time in the world, then suddenly, none. But the minutes and hours and days pass with a more certain rhythm and regularity for his twin brother, Noel. Things tend to come and go more easily for him. He understands how to *wait* for things. "It's what makes him a good driver and a good poker player too," my husband says. "He knows how to anticipate." I like to think that he and I share this sense of measure, and maybe, because the flow of the river is evidence of that measure in the natural world, watching it is to be reassured.

We took our time swimming across the Current, drifting down it and then swimming up it, and finally across it, a fluid boundary that was easily breached. Twenty minutes passed, maybe thirty, and when we finally were on the other side, we found a submerged rock to sit on. One of the advantages of traveling with someone who has spent time on the stage is that it is entirely possible that they will break out into some Shakespeare at unexpected moments. Which happened now. On our perch on the far side of the river, Onni quoted from *As You Like It* a reverie on the rewards of finding a comfortable habitat in a woodland arcadia. "And this our life, exempt from public haunt, Finds tongues in trees, books in the running brooks, Sermons in stone, and good in every thing. I would not change it." This is an approximation, but it's close enough, with an allusive quality as though a few words will lead naturally to the rest.

Talk elsewhere on the river was just as truncated. While the river was not quite crowded that late afternoon, it had other tenants, and in the course of our swim back, we had assorted, abbreviated conversations with the tubers and canoers who drifted by us. "Have you got any idea where the boat launch is?" asked an elderly man who somehow did not seem out of place despite the porkpie hat he had chosen to wear while floating downstream in a yellow and red checkered inner tube. "I've been out here for hours, and I feel like I'm never going to get there." Moments later, a canoer asked me sympathetically whether no one had ever thought to tell me that it's easier to swim downstream than up. The advice was purely rhetorical, but strangely comforting. Maybe because the river itself and the banks on either side are such a gracious and hospitable landscape, they invite the same easy affability in their human occupants. For whatever reason, there seemed to be some consensus that acknowledging one another's presence was only cordial. A few words were enough. Then the words got lost in the river.

That sense of connectivity became even more fantastic as we set up our tent later that evening. We may have been exempt from public haunt, but this was a campground, and the families at the adjoining site had come with a gang of kids. The kids' natural curiosity and the commiseration that is established among campers when the weather threatens to turn led to a camaraderie, and it wasn't long before the kids were bringing us armloads of firewood. When we asked them to tell us their names, they complied with shyness, except for one of the girls, who declared her full name with assurance. "Kathy Jo Bush," she said. When I exclaimed that we shared a surname, she got her dad, and as can happen under such circumstances, we discussed the possibility of our genealogical proximity to the current president. When I suggested the chances were slim, he went on to tell me how it might also be possible from his own research that we were both related to Jesse James. "One makes the law, one breaks it," he concluded and shrugged with cheerful acceptance of the fact that our lineage might touch upon the significant bases of the American judicial system.

I know there is an exact science to the practice of identifying one's ancestry, yet it often seems to me to be governed most by whom we hope to be tied to, tenuous as that tie may be. I remember once seeing a bogus family tree of my own that alleged a tie to Eleanor of Aquitaine, a claim whose implausibility was matched only by its sheer bravado. And here was another possible relative claiming Jesse James. Is it a deficiency of nerve rather than standard of truthfulness that is going to prevent me from claiming this unlikely pair of ancestors? Who's to say. It's only human to speculate on those unknown tributaries in our lineage that make us who we are. And even once some semblance of lineage may seem to have been established, genetic screenings using DNA commonly turn up with other surprises, far-flung ancestral roots that may stretch to ethnicities and races on the other side of the world. I am reminded of the speculative lore suggesting that the water from Big Springs streams down from distant lakes in Montana. Encountering the possibility of a genealogical link, along with the various fantastic conjectures it led to, at the Big Springs campground made me think that our own sources are every bit as mysterious and unknowable as the course and contours of the ancient, subterranean streams that supply the Current River.

Kathy Jo came back after her father had left, and took in what we had boiling over the fire. Ramen noodles, as we had chosen a swim over a trip to the grocery store in Van Buren. "That looks good," she said. "I like spaghetti. More than what we're having anyway." Obligingly, we asked what that might be, and she told us, "Butt. Not human. Cow. But I still don't like it much." And so, although we were not really set up for dinner guests, we asked the eight-year-old girl to join us. As it turned out, Kathy Jo had a well-developed and even slightly ceremonial method of using chopsticks. She held one in each hand, then deployed them expertly together to transport a single strand of dangling noodle, one at a time, from plate to mouth. "Well," I told her, "I've learned two things tonight. I've learned that we may be related, and I've learned a new way to use chopsticks." Unimpressed, she stared at me, appraising the kinds of things I consider worth knowing. Finally she asked, "You know what my favorite thing to do is? I like to learn something. And then I like to relearn it all over again."

The drizzle we woke up to turned into a steadier rain throughout the morning. Hurricane Dennis was hammering the Gulf Coast, and speculation in the campground was that for the first time in forty years the storm would roll up the Mississippi Valley. This was, apparently, good news; campers, I had by then discovered, have a fanaticism fueled by a strong sense of denial, and rather than watch tents being pulled up and folded, I found myself watching piles of firewood grow and tents being shored up with layer upon layer of ripstop polyethylene tarps and nylon dropcloths and awnings. But if hurricane-force winds and a churning rain were cause for enterprise among the campers, I was succumbing to a more dumb depression; whereas a day earlier, the cascade of water from an unknown source had seemed sustaining, cause for wonderment even, today more water, coming unexpectedly from an anomaly of a storm, had soured my mood. More water now seemed dangerous, even treacherous excess. In our own tent, the rain was seeping inexplicably up through the groundcloth in its own small but spiteful pantomime of the underground channels elsewhere in the park, and the already tiny square of dry ground on which my inflatable camping mat sat was diminishing by the minute. Things didn't get much better when we drove into Van Buren for coffee. "What do you do around here on a rainy day?" we asked the cashier, and she laughed and suggested we go to "the mall," by which she meant the dollar store at the other end of main street. It was the same unabashed cheerfulness of the campers shoring up their nylon tents, and by this time I was willing to see it as the cloying pathology of the perpetually optimistic.

Instead, we headed back to the campground, and despite the rain decided to follow a walking trail that took us from the spring down to the river. It had been a dry summer thus far, and the level of the water was down, leaving parts of the riverbank exposed. Its path was more defined than it would be in a wet season, articulated all the more by the composition of rocks and gravel beaches along the banks. The trail meandered up a ridge above the river, through woods of hickory, white oak, and dogwood, and from that vantage point, the circuitous character of the river revealed itself. The Current River is not a straight river; it bends and meanders constantly, finds hollows along the shoreline, redirects itself momentarily, then bends to another turn in the landscape. Yet all the while, its surprises are gentle ones—there are few dramatic changes in depth, few unexpected rapids or drops. Below us we could see the spot at which the clear creek from the spring joins the river itself, and even that confluence of water from beneath the earth with the water that streams along its surface is easy; here is a place where the confluence of the known and the unknown appears effortless.

Austere cabins were scattered along the ridge, and I found myself plotting various ruses to persuade Onni to pull up our little wet tent and relocate to one of these. Just as she had been unfazed by the rat snake at the Delaware River three years earlier, the rain today did nothing to discourage her. When we stopped to take in a view of the river at an overlook at the top of the trail, we heard the voice of a man in one of the cabins. He was arguing, it seemed, with his teenage son, and in what sounded to be a common case of cabin fever, he was demanding an apology for some infraction. Moments later he came out of the cabin with an exasperated look on his face and walked out to look at the river and let it do its work. He had been coming here for years with his family, he told us. He had a yellow Labrador at his side, and he told us that the dog sometimes floated down the river in its own inner tube with the rest of the family. And then he told us that one of the things he liked to do most was to put on his scuba gear so he could sit on the bottom of the river, just looking up at the water streaming overhead and at the kayakers and canoers paddling over him. "They probably know I'm there," he added. "You can see the bubbles." And already, just thinking of this, the tone of his voice and the tension in his face from the argument with his son had softened.

Had circumstances been different, it might just as well have been me being caught in an argument with a teenage boy, and I envied him for having found such a salve to the petty frustrations of domestic life; sitting quietly at the bottom of a clear river was not something I had ever considered, and for all its eccentricity, it seemed a wise way to confront one's catalog of ordinary worries. The accounts of sports technology being put to innovative uses usually have to do with athletes being able to go faster or farther or higher. But here was sports technology being put to a different kind of extreme—extreme solitude, perhaps, or extreme repose or extreme solace—and I knew then that going to the river accommodates some elusive contradiction of being at a remove and being fully engaged as well; it is a way to get away from life, and at the same time, a way to become reconnected to it. It is unlikely that the poet Matthew Arnold ever imagined a man spending a July afternoon sitting on the bottom of the river, but still, he seems to have found a way to write about the experience a century and a half ago: "Below the surface stream, shallow and light, / Of what we say and feel—below the stream, / As light, of what we think we feel, there flows / With noiseless current, strong, obscure and deep, / The central stream of what we feel indeed."

The hurricane never quite materialized, but in its place came a softer drizzle, and talking Onni into taking up residence in one of the cabins was not the struggle I had imagined. The cabins were primitive, in the rustic manner of the National Park Service, with pine walls and simple screen windows, and the sound of the rain on the leaves throughout the night seemed like natural acoustics for these small shelters. Along with the trails and roads in this park, the cabins had been built in the thirties by the Civilian Conservation Corps, a jobs program initiated by Franklin Roosevelt as part of the New Deal, and in the stone lodge where we had arranged to take the cabin for the night were old photographs of the boys who were part of that corps. For about thirty dollars a month, the boys cleared trails and built roads, hung telephone lines, and constructed the stone walkways that wind through the park and the small shingled cabins. The captions next to the photographs told us how these boys from the Missouri and Arkansas woods also often learned to read and have table manners and function in society outside of their families while they did this work. Sometime that night, my dreams took me to the province of the young, and images of those country boys building roads in the forest morphed into the teenager arguing with his dad, and then into my own sixteen-year-old sons building a ramp for their skateboards with swooping bends and curves that would catapult them into some world that was fast and easy and full of grace. I woke up, finally, in a state of wonderment at all the ways young men find to make the world inhabitable, all the ways they manage to clear a little space and find some path through the anarchy they see around them.

The rain hadn't let up, so later that morning we drove up to Blue Spring simply so that we could see another of the Current's sources. A guidebook I picked up along the way had this to say: "Missouri is home to nine Blue Springs, two Blue Hole Springs, two Blue Grass Springs, a Blue Lick, and a Blue Stem Spring. But the Blue Spring on the Current River sets the standard for all of them and for blue water everywhere." Another visitor to the spring whom we passed on the path put it differently, saying simply, "I've never seen a color like it." When we got to the spring itself, I realized I couldn't say whether it was a blue I had never before seen or the truest blue I had ever seen.

Probably both were true. A small animal was swimming directly across the pool, sleek and streamlined, its brown fur slicked back. Later I learned it was a mink, a fact that only added to the sheer, implausible extravagance of the place. At the time, though, its identity was unknown to me, as was the depth of the pool, its strange flora, its origins.

We decided to drive back to Big Spring for another swim in the Current River. It was still drizzling, but as Kathy Jo said, sometimes you just want to learn something and then relearn it all over again. Sometimes it seems what makes the world a place of comfort is the way things repeat themselves. Or one thing can remind you of another in a way that infuses both things with a little more meaning. If you can do the same thing long enough or repeat it enough times, you may find that your purpose changes. The same simple act can accommodate a multitude of intents. Maybe this is the meaning and value of rituals. I don't know. But I *do* know that crossing a river began as a way to breach a divide. Later, it came to include the possibility of being swept away. And sometime later still, these two objectives began to converge. Sometimes it is possible to find knowledge through nothing more than familiarity. It's the way the lines of a nineteenth-century poet can reveal something about a man sitting at the bottom of a river; or the way a natural spring in the Ozarks is an iteration of a cut-glass inkwell; or the way you will look at blue water a hundred or a thousand times in your life before you discover how blue it can truly be; or just the way the name of a river can repeat itself.

I think of that index of the unknown that we all carry with us. I haven't the faintest idea about what kind of lives my sons will lead, though as with most parents, that often seems like the thing that matters most. Nor do I have any idea about how my own life will play out or where, though at fifty-two, that information suddenly seems more important to me than it has before. And I think of all the mysteries of intention and desire that keep us wondering about even those people we know best. While we may persist in guessing at our own sources and origins, it is not the mysteries of what has already happened that are of the greatest concern, but those of the future, how long we will live and where we may die and how our children will fare. If the Current River and all its blue, blue springs have a gift, it is to suggest that those unknown areas in our lives, whether past or future, can also be places of grace and enchantment.

Afterword

Usually when I begin to think about a book, one of the first steps is to get organized, to apply some kind of order and structure to the piles of notes I have made over the years, to find some system in which to file the articles, clippings, and photographs I have collected, and to encourage and otherwise coerce all this information into finding its rightful place. Eventually, the hope is, some kind of sensible narrative will emerge, and the story will find a form. That strategy only went so far here.

Of course, my experience at each river was specific to that river. Each river has its own lore, its own history, its own flow, and its own narrative flow, and for a little while it seemed as though it might be easy to know what particular information accompanied each river. But the more I swam and the more I wrote, the more information I kept finding that had no natural home. Stuck in a book about the Connecticut River was a photograph of a painting by Paula Scher, who paints maps of real places that are streaming with typography and have somehow been reconfigured in her mind and by her hand into some geographic wonderland of place-names and landscape. "Who does not have that chronologically disorienting feeling that uncharted territories are growing at a faster rate than our ability to map them?" the reviewer asked. I find a quote by the art historian John Ruskin, who tells me, "All rivers, small or large, agree in one character, they like to lean a little on one side: they cannot bear to have their channels deepest in the middle, but will always, if they can, have one bank to sun themselves upon, and another to get cool under; one shingly shore to play over, where they may be shallow, and foolish, and childlike, and another steep shore, under which they can pause and purify themselves, and get the strength of their waves fully together for due occasion. Rivers in this way are just like wise men, who keep one side of their life for play, and another for work." Did I find this true more in one river than another? I asked myself.

And there was a swimming manual from the twenties with diagrams for different strokes and carefully calibrated equations having to do with body weight, the pressure of the water, buoyancy, and what it is, exactly, that allows a person to float. Elsewhere is a picture I ripped from a magazine of the work of the photographer Richard Misrach. The lone swimmer, photographed from the balcony of a hotel in Hawaii, is traversing a vast ocean of green. The photographer omitted the horizon line, and something about this image of solitude in the water is familiar to me. Elsewhere still are the phone numbers and e-mail addresses of swimmers whose names I was given because their journeys in some ways intersect with mine. But none of these words or images or numbers followed a direct course to any single river. Instead, they streamed from one river to another and another.

But if the system for cataloging this assorted material did not come to me then, months later I came across a logical, if impractical, system that seemed as though it might provide some way to fasten these thoughts and images together. I did not find it at my desk, but more unexpectedly during a walk along Dennings Point, a small peninsula that juts out into the Hudson River just below Beacon, New York. Dennings Point is one of those small places that has managed to accumulate an extensive history; over the centuries, its sixty-five acres have gone from forest to farmland to industry; it has been the site of a Native American settlement, a colonial outpost, a Victorian estate, a brickworks, a commercial fishery. Alexander Hamilton lived on the point during the American Revolution, in the hopes of receiving a field command from Washington across the river in New Windsor. During his tenure there, he wrote letters and editorials, and the ideals he considered there were later reflected in the Federalist Papers, which set out many of the ideas that came to form the American Constitution. And in the early twenty-first century, the Beacon Institute for Rivers and Estuaries is planning on building its campus on the point, adapting some of the old industrial buildings there for its center for research, policy, and education about rivers, estuaries, and society.

But the fragment of the point's varied history that captured my imagination most that afternoon were some vestiges of its industrial past that I encountered near the site where a paper clip factory had once stood. Not far from the old factory I came across what must have been the remnants of a storage shed. The debris there included little scraps of powdery, rusted clips that evaporated when touched, the frayed vestiges of the huge coils of wire that had been used to make the clips, and scattered on the ground all around were big, irregularly shaped blocks of clips that had seemed to coalesce into each other, condensed and compressed by decades of being exposed to the weather and decomposing into one another, forming some sort of strange improvisational sculpture.

The Dia:Beacon museum is less than a mile away, housed in a renovated old cookie carton factory, and these randomly formed chunks of matter might have been some exercise in conceptual sculpture that had somehow been misplaced, ending up in the industrial space that had *not* been reinvented as a modern art museum. Because why couldn't this qualify as a piece of art? There is something basic and essential about a paper clip, a little piece of twisted wire that nonetheless manages, with economy, efficiency, and simplicity, to keep things together. And these chunks of thousands upon thousands of them melded together seemed to be some kind of expression of ultimate connectivity. And while I know the manufacturing of paper clips came long after the American Revolution, it seemed logical that these accessories of fastening were fabricated on a site where Alexander Hamilton had once framed his thoughts on how people could best govern themselves in society.

Today, the Beacon Institute for Rivers and Estuaries plans to use the footprint of the old paper clip factory when it builds its labs, education and training centers for the study of green building design and technologies. It's fitting that the place where the most basic tool of fastening was manufactured has now evolved into a place of learning; sometimes, the material world makes complete and beautiful sense. But even beyond that, the archive of little clips on the bank of the Hudson River was a kind of physical manifestation of the multitude of streams in the current itself, as it ripples and curls in and around on itself and fastens one thought and one idea and one feeling to another and another and another. And certainly these powdery, ancient clips seemed the ideal accessory for all the disparate information scattered for so many months across my desk.

Rivers offer us this multiplicity of meaning. And people are drawn to water and swimming for the same infinite variety of reasons they come up with to justify any other human enterprise. In his meditation on swimming, *Haunts of the Black Masseur: The Swimmer as Hero,* the English writer Charles Sprawson catalogs some of them. "Swimming, like opium, can cause a sense of detachment from ordinary life," he suggests, and indeed, for Thomas de Quincey, swimming was analogous to smoking opium; in eliciting a sense of weightlessness and immersion, swimming unleashed the creative imagination. And in the novels of D. H. Lawrence, swimming provides "brief moments of male happiness, a symbolic release from sexual inhibition, unhappy marriages, and frustrated love." Goethe, on the other hand, once wrote, "I went into the water and drowned my overwrought imagination." Gaston Bachelard was content to remain on the banks, saying simply, "My pleasure still is to follow the stream, to walk along its banks in the right direction, in the direction of the flowing water, the water that leads life towards the next village." Escape, clarity, pure pleasure—who can deny that these all serve as powerful incentives for anything.

That same plurality of vision showed up in a 2003 exhibit called "The American River." The juror Carl Belz wrote of the varying perspectives that the artists represented had of the river. The paintings, photographs, and drawings documented the river from myriad perspectives; some seemed to immerse the viewer in the ripples of water and light, while others took a more distant view, placing the river at a great remove and suggesting the distance we have put ourselves from nature. There is not one river, Belz suggested, but many, and he wrote that for many artists "reverie takes place at a great distance from the river, reminding us of nature's vast and irresistible embrace; others, at the same time, bring us close enough to visually caress the river's sparkling surface or glimpse intimately the secluded pools where the fish might lie; and yet another group, I'm thinking here of abstractionists, appear to immerse us in the river itself, surrounding us completely with its shifting light and color and its constant movement."

And I think, too, of Christo's proposal of the river as a shining roof rippling overhead. Or of a piece of sculpture I once saw by the artists Emily Puthoff and Elena Sniezek. They had positioned two small bowls on a table, and through some manner of electronic wizardry, the bottom of each bowl had been outfitted with a small LCD screen flickering with the image of rippling water. But whether it is the river as a roof or the river as a continuous drink that can be found in a small bowl, that range of perspectives is not restricted to artists; it was also what I looked for and found over the years as the water in these rivers became a lens not only for all the different ways in which things can become clear, but for the benefits of obscurity; for what danger, fear, and beauty could mean in the course of one's life, for how the alternating currents of solitude and anonymity can inform the way one lives, and for all the ways that an appreciation of mystery and uncertainty can infuse even the most mundane routines.

Rivers offer an obvious metaphor for an individual life, but at the same time they offer escape from it. There is some part of swimming that allows you to be someone else. Once, many years ago, I parachuted out of a plane. It was a weekend excursion, done purely for fun. A friend and I drove out to an airport in New Jersey, where we spent the morning in a training course, which taught us how to step out of the plane at three thousand feet, where to position our feet and our arms, when to let go of the plane's struts, when to pull open the chute, and how to touch ground, then bend our knees to fall. And then in midafternoon, we went up and jumped. This outing was, of course, fully documented with photographs. Like the tourists at the Great Pyramid or the Great Wall of China, we wanted a visual witness to our proximity to the great monument, or in this case, the great beyond.

Several weeks later, my photograph arrived, and with some excitement, I tore open the envelope to see just what I looked like in midair. Different, it seemed. Actually, very different. The photographer had apparently confused my identification number with that of another fledgling parachutist, and the photograph I received was the picture of a complete stranger. Which, I eventually realized, had its own kind of logic. Three thousand feet in the air, the earth, or the entire state of new Jersey at least, was a distant reality, and for those few minutes, this was a new sensation, a new view, a new perspective on life at large, and there was no way not to feel like a different person. It was possible, for a brief time, to be outside of myself. As happens in the moments after any extraordinary, new experience, I was, for an instant, a stranger to myself. It is a sensation offered to most of us at one time or another in our lives, and for me, swimming in rivers granted it often and generously.

Swimming in rivers can also be a way of sightseeing. A friend of mine who is an editor is also a swimmer. She has a summer house in Wellfleet, Massachusetts, and she has made it her project to swim across as many ponds as she can in that town. It's a different way to look at buildings, she tells me; it offers a different view of land, houses, people. And I wonder if this view, or rather, her search for this view, is also what makes her a skilled editor. I would suspect also that the information she gets on her swims is somehow assimilated in a fluid manner; or that it becomes absorbed in her thinking in some kind of organic, fluid process.

I imagine sometimes, too, that the lure rivers have had in my own life is simply an echo of childhood experience. When I was young, my family would spend part of each summer with my grandparents who lived on Cape Cod. And in the afternoons, my mother and my sister and I would often walk down to a small beach at the inlet near the house. My sister and I usually swam closer to the shore, but we would watch as our mother swam halfway across the bay to a white buoy. These were languid summer swims, but her strokes were long and sure, and she swam straight, as though following a direct path from the dock. But although we often talked of it, she never swam the mile or so across the entire bay, and I sometimes wonder if my own compulsion to swim across rivers is a way of helping my mother complete her swims.

But the closest I have ever really come to understanding the compulsion to swim was found not in any of the narratives of swimmers, nor in ancient legend, nor in pictorial representations of water. Rather, I found it in a caption. Like anything else in life, the answer to big questions is often to be found in a small place. I was at the Museum of Modern Art in New York City, looking at a painting by the French artist Yves Klein, who is known especially for the deep cobalt hue he used in much of his work. Klein was said to have been inspired by the brilliant blue of the Mediterranean sky and sea, and International Klein Blue, or IKB, is a deep vibrant ultramarine hue that the painter created by suspending the pigment in a clear synthetic resin that heightened its depth and intensity. It was a color that he applied to a broad range of human experience: to ordinary household objects, to monochromatic paintings; and in his body painting, or *anthropométries,* he drenched women's bodies in the paint, then instructed them to lie and roll around on the canvas, leaving their imprints. Once, in the eighties, the Guggenheim Museum went so far in an exhibition of Klein's work as to install a shallow box filled with the brilliant blue pigment; the box took up almost the entire ground floor of the museum, so that when you looked down from the spiraling floors above, you found yourself staring into what seemed a radiant pond of blue pigment.

There is no indication that Yves Klein was a fanatic swimmer, so I can only suppose that he was a frustrated one. Who else on earth would insist that this color infiltrate all of life: household sponges, coffee tables, canvas, women's bodies? At the Museum of Modern Art, the caption next to the monochromatic painting read: "This ultramarine blue, named International Klein Blue, is inextricably linked with Yves Klein. Preoccupied with spirituality, Klein adopted this heavenly blue as a means of evoking immateriality and boundlessness."

I don't think the water in any of the rivers I have ever swum in has come close to having quite the clarity or vibrance of IKB. Each river is distinguished by its own taste, texture, flavor, color. The Hudson tends to be a softer, more subtle green gray, flecked with brown, and it is the very lack of clarity that speaks to its aquatic health. The afternoon I went to the Delaware it was a darker emerald color, but, still, it captured the full radiance of the afternoon light. The fine silt of the Connecticut River gave that water a texture and materiality. And all of these, eventually, became a template for me for going forward. Often, at the start of *something,* it became useful for me to imagine what kind of river I was stepping into: Was it one that required stepping in cautiously, feeling my way over the stones, or one with a clearer bed? What was the nature of the shallows, the sediment, the sand? Was the current gentle and lazy or faster and more unpredictable? What kind of watchfulness was required, what needed to be observed?

Then there are all the rivers I will probably never swim in. Sometimes late at night when I am driving from Manhattan to my home in the Hudson Valley, I take the FDR Drive, and on my right is the East River, a slender ribbon of black water with a treacherous current, an oil slick of river ablaze with reflections of city lights. But even that is a reminder of something a little bit wild streaming along the margin of the night.

None of these rivers are electric blue, and I wouldn't know about the spirituality Yves Klein had in mind. But all that said, immateriality and boundlessness sound about right.

Acknowledgments

In books, as in rivers, one thing leads to another. My thanks first, then, to Myron Adams, who said one day in spring 2001, "Sure, let's take a swim across the Hudson. There's nothing to it." I am as grateful to Ann LaFarge, who continued to ask about each swim and each river, and to my agent, Albert LaFarge, who understood about rivers and believed in this book from the beginning. At Bloomsbury, I am indebted to my editor, Gillian Blake, for her skill, insight, and, not least, her instinct for brevity; and to Benjamin Adams for his patience and efficiency. People who love rivers and are committed to their safekeeping love to talk about them too, and I am enormously thankful to everyone mentioned in these pages. I owe thanks as well to Dr. David L. Strayer at the Institute of Ecosystem Studies; Dr. Frank Nickell at Southeast Missouri State University; Keith Pitzer, Evan Hansen, Joseph Cocalis, and Bethia Waterman at the Hudson River Estuary Program. Melanie Marder Parks's maps chart these rivers anew, and I am fortunate to have them. Kim Ima at La MaMa E.T.C. used pieces of this in *Travels, Tours & One-Night Stands*, and I am grateful to her for her grace and skill. Thanks as well to Emily Adams, Jon DeVries, and Christina Svane, who joined me in some of these rivers. I am grateful to friends who reviewed early pages, especially Anne Kreamer, trusted adviser always, and Greg Furman, laplane colleague and friend. Thanks as well to the Army Corps of

Engineers, who never failed to discourage me from getting into these rivers, yet always concluded by saying, "Good luck to you." And my gratitude, as always, to Brian, Noel, and Luc, and of course, finally, for being there, to Onni.

A Note on the Author

Akiko Busch is the author of *Geography of Home* and *The Uncommon Life of Common Objects*. She writes regularly about design and culture, and lives in the Hudson Valley with her husband and two sons.